Y0-ABF-075

# Contents

# An Interpretation of the King Kwanggaet'o Inscription

*By Takashi Hatada*
SENSHU UNIVERSITY
*Translated by V. Dixon Morris*
UNIVERSITY OF HAWAII

## 1. Background of the Inscription

The King Kwanggaet'o inscription is a memorial on a stele erected at the tomb of King Kwanggaet'o, whose full, proper name was Kukkangsang Kwanggaet'ogyŏng p'yŏngan hot'ae-wang. Kwanggaet'o is an abbreviation. The same man was also referred to as King Hot'ae and sometimes as Great King Yŏngnak, after the era name Yŏngnak, which he selected. He was the nineteenth monarch of the kingdom of Koguryŏ and reigned during the twenty-two years from A.D. 391 to 412. Though he was only thirty-nine years old at the time of his death, he nonetheless extended his boundaries in all directions and left behind a greater Koguryŏ kingdom.

The memorial stele was erected in 414, two years after his death. Its location is in the present People's Republic of China, outside the capital of Chian District, T'unghua Special Area, Chilin Province. It is not far from the banks of the Yalu River along its middle reaches. The Chian District was the site of the Koguryŏ capital.[1]

The stele is an irregular rectangular column made of natural stone. It is 6.2 meters high, and at the base its width on side one is 1.55 meters; on side two, 1.44 meters; side three, 1.97 meters; and side four, 1.39 meters. Characters have been carved on the four sides. There are forty-four lines of writing with eleven lines on side one, ten lines on side two, fourteen on side three, and nine on side four. Each line of writing contains forty-one characters, except the sixth line on side one, which has

---

1. Koguryŏ moved the seat of the capital in the year 427 A.D.

two blanks at the end of the line. This makes a total of 1,802 characters in the inscription.[2] Of these, 260 characters are completely illegible owing to damage to the surface of the stele, and there are many other characters that cannot be read precisely.[3]

In terms of content, one can divide the inscription into three major sections. The first section begins with the foundation myth of the ancestral King Ch'umo, extols the great deeds of King Kwanggaet'o, and records the reasons for erecting the stele to commemorate the king. Section two records in chronological order Kwanggaet'o's military exploits, that is, his victories in wars of conquest. These include seven wars: (1) the subjugation of the Pi-li in 395 (the Pi-li seem to have been a Khitan people from the upper reaches of the Liao River); (2) the subjugation of Paekche in 396; (3) the defeat in 398 of the Po-shen (who were apparently a Su-shen people from the Mutan River); (4) the dispatch in 400 of troops to the southern end of the Korean peninsula to subjugate the Wa, who had invaded Silla; (5) the defeat in 404 of Wa armies that had invaded Taebang (near Hwanghae Province); (6) the dispatch of troops in 407 to a place that is unclear since the characters spelling out the area are missing (there are various theories: Paekche or perhaps the Hou-yen from the Liaotung area); (7) the subjugation in 410 of the Tung-fu-yü (who are variously said to have been in North Hamgyŏng Province or in the Nungan-Ch'angch'un area of Manchuria). Section three records in detail the number of households of the gravekeepers, grouped by place of origin.

As stated earlier, the stele was erected in the second year following the king's death, but in the years that followed, its existence was completely forgotten. There was absolutely no document from either Korea or China that recorded the content of the inscription.[4] Moreover, following the destruction of Koguryŏ, the area reverted to wilderness so that visitors there were few, and for centuries the stele was lost.[5]

Then in the latter half of the nineteenth century, reclamation of the area commenced, and the Ch'ing government of China created the Huai-jen District in 1876 as the political institution for the control of the area.

---

2. There are different views on the number of lines as well as the number of letters. There is a view that an additional line existed between sides one and two, but this has not been proven. There is also a view that the total number of letters was not forty-one; that is, that there were no letters on top of lines nine and ten on side two.

3. Owing to the severe damage to the stele, the same character is often read differently by different people.

4. The inscription is recorded in a Japanese book, Nan'ensho, but this is a bogus book written in modern times.

5. On occasion, travelers saw the stele, and sometimes they took note of the large stone monument, but few observed the inscription on the stele.

Ultimately, farmers who were opening the land to cultivation discovered the stele; they reported their find to the magistrate of Huaijen District, and that official investigated. This seems to have been in the late 1870s or early 1880s. The stele was overgrown with vegetation, but the official burned it off and so discovered the characters hidden beneath. He made a copy by placing paper over the surface of the inscription and tracing by hand the outline of the characters, a technique known as *sōkōbon*, which differs from a rubbing in which the paper is placed over the inscription and rubbed with ink to produce an impression. Afterward, he filled in all but the outlines with ink.

This outline tracing technique is inaccurate compared to the rubbing technique, but it is used when the original is extremely uneven in texture as a result of surface damage. In any event, by using this technique it became clear that the inscription celebrated the deeds of King Kwanggaet'o, and the existence of the stele came to light once again, some 1,500 years after it had been erected in 414.

Later, when the inscription became famous, rubbings were made that were more accurate than the original outline tracing. The first rubbings were made in the latter half of the 1880s, and many other rubbings were made from then until the end of World War II and have been preserved in Japan, China, and Korea.

## 2. The Development of Research on the Inscription

The first copy of the King Kwanggaet'o inscription was, as stated earlier, that made by the Ch'ing official of Huaijen District. In the course of events, this was transmitted to central officials in China and came to the attention of Chinese scholars. Later, when rubbings—as opposed to outline tracings—were made, the interest of Chinese scholars heightened, and research on the inscription made progress.[6]

Those who expressed the strongest interest in the inscription, however, were the Japanese. A copy made by outline tracing found its way to Japan as early as 1884 or 1885, only a few years after the stele's rediscovery. The person who brought it was Sakao Kagenobu, an army officer and intelligence agent of the Japanese General Staff Office who was investigating conditions in Manchuria and China. He had gone to China in 1880, had travelled about, and had gone to Chian District, where the

6. In China, Wang Chih-hsiu, Chen Wen-ch'ao, Jung Hsi, Yang Shou-ching, Lo Chen-yü, Yeh Ch'ang-chih, and other scholars studied the inscription. They were scholars of the late Ch'ing period. After the fall of the Ch'ing dynasty, there were no studies by Chinese scholars. Among Europeans, E. Chavannes visited Chian in 1907 and published photographs of the stele and the inscription in "Les Monuments de l'Ancien Royaume Coréen de Kao-keou-li," *T'oung Pao,* 2d ser., 9 (1908).

King Kwanggaet'o stele was situated. He conducted an on-site investigation and acquired a copy of the tracing. In 1884 or 1885, he returned to Japan with his copy and turned it over to the General Staff Office.[7] These were the circumstances, then, that brought the inscription to Japan so very early.

The General Staff was fascinated by the inscription and began research on it within the Staff Office. Historians, aside from those of the army, were also invited to participate, and in 1889, after several years of study, they published their findings. These appeared under the authorship of Yokoi Tadanao in number five of the journal *Kaiyoroku* and included articles entitled "On the Ancient Koguryŏ Inscription," "The Excavation of the Koguryŏ Stele," "An Interpretation of the Koguryŏ Inscription," and "The Ancient Koguryŏ Inscription," which was a photograph of the tracing. Yokoi Tadanao was a professor at the military academy and director of the inscription research within the General Staff Office.

Thus, it was an intelligence agent who first brought the transcription of the King Kwanggaet'o inscription to Japan, and the first to study it was the army General Staff Office. One must also understand that at the time, the Japanese army was extremely interested in moving onto the continent, and though Japan was still weak and overbalanced in Korea by the Chinese, it was planning ways to move into Korea and Manchuria and therefore was making efforts to promote military preparedness.

In this transcription the term "Wa" appeared. As we saw earlier, the Wa people entered the Korean scene as opponents of King Kwanggaet'o of Koguryŏ and fought him. Since these Wa were thought to be Japanese, a Japanese army planning a continental advance found in this a powerful source of historical rationalization for their contemporary ambitions. This was the reason for the extraordinary energy the General Staff devoted to research on the inscription.

The *Nihon shoki,* a history compiled in Japan in the eighth century, recorded that the ancient emperors of Japan had sent armies to Korea, subjugated the various countries there, and controlled the peninsula through a so-called Mimana Nihon Fu (Japanese Office in Mimana). Most Japanese believed this to be a fact, and so when the General Staff learned of the activities of the Wa from the King Kwanggaet'o stele, they associated these Wa with the imperial government of ancient Japan and believed they had found corroboration of the *Nihon shoki* account. Thus, they believed Korea had originally been Japanese territory.

7. The personal history of Sakao Kagenobu was recorded for the first time in 1972 by Saeki Arikyo in his article "Kokaido ōryō hibun saikentō no tameno josho, Sanbo honbu to Chōsen kenkyū," in *Nihon rekishi,* no. 287.

The fact that the Kwanggaet'o inscription had first been studied by the General Staff placed limits on the directions that subsequent research on the inscription could take in Japan. After publication of the General Staff's findings in 1889, many historians were attracted to the inscription and several new publications followed.[8] These new studies found errors in parts of the army's research and developed improved transcripts of the text, since later, rubbings, rather than tracings, were brought over.[9] And there were also Japanese scholars who had opportunities to visit the site and to examine the stele *in situ*. In fact, many such Japanese were able to go to the site after Japanese victories in the Sino-Japanese War (1894–1895) and the Russo-Japanese War (1904–1905). These included such outstanding scholars as Torii Ryūzō, Sekino Tei, Imanishi Ryū, and Kuroita Katsumi, all of whom visited the site at various times and investigated the stele.[10] Moreover, following the creation of Manchukuo in 1932, Manchuria came completely under Japanese control so that it was easy for Japanese to go to the Chian area, and many went as sightseers to the Kwanggaet'o stele. More scholarly studies of the inscription and the remains also flourished.[11]

Through the participation of such specialists, research on the inscription developed apace. More accurate rubbings were made, and readings and interpretations of the text became more precise. These new works reached a far higher level than that of the earlier General Staff studies. Nonetheless, these more careful studies done by scholars did not refute the conclusions of the General Staff's work. Certainly, they uncovered any number of gaps in the transcribed text used by the General Staff as well as many errors of reading and interpretation. But the basic findings were confirmed, indeed, strengthened. By basic findings I mean the consensus that the imperial government of ancient Japan sent troops to Korea, subjugated Paekche and Silla, and fought Koguryŏ. At the same time, because of this interpretation, the existence of the "Mimana Nihon Fu" mentioned in the *Nihon shoki* was also accepted as a historical fact. Thus, despite the many partial revisions, the conclusions published by the General Staff were essentially unchanged.

8. Kan Masatomo, "Kōrai kōtaiō hikō," *Shigakkai zasshi* 2, nos. 22, 23, 24, and 25 (1891). Naka Michiyo, "Kōkuri kohikō," *Shigakkai zasshi* 4, nos. 47, 48, and 49 (1893). Miyake Yonekichi, "Kōrai kohikō," *Kokogaku zasshi* 2, nos. 1, 2, and 3 (1898); idem, "Kōrai kohikō tsuika," ibid. 2, no. 5 (1898).

9. The original rubbing of the inscription was first used by Miyake Yonekichi in his second article "Kōrai kohikō tsuika." However, the whereabouts of this rubbing is not known.

10. Torii visited the stele in 1905, 1909, and 1913; Sekino and Imanishi visited it in 1913; and Kuroita visited the place in 1918.

11. In 1935, Ikeuchi Hiroshi, Hamada Kōsaku, Fujita Ryōsaku, Umehara Matsuji, and others visited the place.

Following the Japanese surrender in World War II, Japan withdrew from Korea and Manchuria, and that meant that the Japanese lost the opportunity to see the stele. Research on the inscription also abated. But the views of it that had formed in the prewar period remained, and these were the views adopted in history texts. Prewar history textbooks were based on the records of the *Nihon shoki* and said that Japan had controlled ancient Korea, whereas postwar texts were based on the King Kwanggaet'o stele inscription but still accepted Japan's control of Korea. Thus the basis for the view that Japan had controlled Korea moved from an unreliable ancient chronicle to the reliable stele inscription. Though the history texts written after the surrender were vastly different from their prewar counterparts,[12] in this one respect there was no change, and the King Kwanggaet'o stele was the basis of the argument.

Korean scholars, however, did not yield to the Japanese view, and they opposed the use of the stele as the basis of the Japanese argument. They had their own understanding, different from that of the Japanese, about how to read and interpret the inscription. In 1955, Chŏng In-bo wrote an article interpreting the inscription,[13] and in 1966 both Pak Si-hyŏng and Kim Sŏk-hyŏng wrote books on the subject.[14] These are among the leading Korean reactions to this issue, and the content of the studies will be dealt with later.

Such Korean reactions notwithstanding, scholarly circles in Japan were not easily persuaded. In 1971, however, Nakatsuka Akira contributed to the debate with a critique of research attitudes toward the Kwanggaet'o inscription. It was he who pointed out that it had been a Japanese intelligence agent who had brought forth the transcript of the inscription in the first place and that it was the General Staff that had first studied it. His critique aimed broadly at the very character of modern Japanese historical scholarship.[15] Then in 1972, Saeki Arikiyo added his own review of Japanese scholarship on the inscription by tracing in detail the career of the agent who brought the text back, Sakao Kage-

12. In textbooks prior to World War Two, the ancient history of Japan was based on the *Nihon shoki.* After the war, some findings resulting from archeological research were incorporated. In the textbooks prior to the war, Japanese ancient history was centered on the emperor, but this was also changed.

13. Chŏng's article was published in 1955, but he seems to have written it somewhat earlier.

14. Pak Si-hyŏng and Kim Sŏk-hyŏng are North Korean scholars. They visited the stele in 1963. This was the only academic investigation of the stele after the war. The rubbing of the inscription taken by these scholars was similar to those taken by Japanese scholars.

15. Nakatsuka Akira, "Nihon shigakushi ni okeru Chōsen mondai, tokuni kōkai do ōryōhi o megutte," *Shisō,* no. 561 (1971).

nobu, and the later research in the General Staff Office. He also analyzed the role that the Japanese army had played in historical research on
Korea in the Meiji period.[16]

At almost the same time, Yi Chin-hŭi, a Korean scholar resident in
Japan, published yet another work, a book on the inscription itself. In
this, he minutely examined the circumstances surrounding the discovery
of the stele, and he studied the numerous tracings, rubbings, and photographs of the Kwanggaet'o inscription, arranged them in chronological
order of production, and then studied evidence of changes in the characters themselves over the years. On the basis of his evidence he argued that
Japanese military officers had effaced the inscription and falsified it in
ways that suited their convenience. Here was a shock! If Yi were right, all
previous research on the inscription would be open to question. Indeed,
the very basis for the argument that ancient Japan had controlled Korea,
which depended on the inscription, would be swept away.

Yi Chin-hŭi's theory caused intense repercussions in scholarly circles, both in Japan and abroad. In Japan, some individuals began to
have second thoughts about the previous research, while others attacked
Yi's theory. All admired his careful studies of the tracings and rubbings,
but thus far no one has fully accepted his contention that Japanese officers falsified the inscription.[17] In Korea, however, despite some opposition, most scholars accept his view and agree that Japanese officers did
change the stele.[18] From the Democratic People's Republic of Korea
there has come no word at all, either for or against the Yi theory. Since
World War II, the only scholars who have had direct access to study the
stele itself have been North Koreans, and one would expect them to express an opinion. But for whatever reason, they have not reacted.

Yi Chin-hŭi's theory casts doubt upon the characters of the inscription itself. If one examines Yi's view carefully, one sees that research
based on the present inscription or on rubbings would be meaningless.
To proceed with research it will be necessary to conduct a scientific in-
quiry concerning the stele itself and to determine which characters have

16. See Saeki's article, "Kokaido ōryō hibun saikento no tameno josho."
17. Japanese scholars do not subscribe to the theory of Yi Chin-hŭi because the falsified
portion that Yi pointed out was relatively short. Had the Japanese falsified the inscription,
they would have made it more favorable to the Japanese, but the inscription made it clear
that the Japanese were defeated. The Japanese might have made an error in copying the inscription, but it is not likely that they consciously falsified it.
18. The impact on Korean academia was significant and many scholars expressed their
opinions. For examples, see the articles that appeared in *Sin tonga,* June 1972; *Chosŏn ilbo,* November 18 and 19, 1972; *Sin tonga,* January 1973; and *Chosŏn ilbo,* January 26,
1973.

been altered. This is essential. However, an on-site investigation of the stele is extremely difficult given the present state of international relations. In the meantime, even though such doubts remain, we have no option but to continue our studies using the previously made rubbings as source material.[19]

### 3. Readings and Interpretations of the Inscription

What has so far been the point at issue between Korean and Japanese scholars with respect to the stele is the portion concerning the activities of the Wa. In chronological order, these are:

A.D. 391   invasion by the Wa.
A.D. 399   Wa aggression against Silla, which appears in the passage in which the Silla king requests aid from Kwanggaet'o.
A.D. 400   Wa defeated by the Koguryŏ army sent in response to the Silla request. On this occasion, the Alla people cooperated with the Wa in fighting the Koguryŏ army.
A.D. 404   Wa invaded Taebang and were defeated by King Kwanggaet'o.

Japanese scholars, seeing these Wa actions, believed that the Wa played an active role in Korea in the late fourth and early fifth centuries. They also regarded the Wa as the Yamato government of Japan and argued that ancient Japan had sent military expeditions to Korea and had controlled Korea.[20]

Japanese scholars especially stressed the invasion of 391. This passage appears on lines eight and nine on the first side of the stele, and it takes this form:

(教遣)         (王躬率)

百残新羅旧是属民由来朝貢
而倭以辛卯年来渡海破百残
羅以為臣民

19. There is little difference between the rubbing of the inscription taken by the North Korean scholars in 1963 (see note 14) and that taken by the Japanese before the war. According to Yi Chin-hŭi's theory, the falsification by Japanese soldiers should have become obvious on closer examination, and different characters from those taken by Japanese scholars should have been found. However, no new characters were revealed, a fact due either to an inadequate investigation by the North Koreans or to an error in Yi's conjecture.

20. A place name, Mimana kara, appears in the account of the battles between the Koguryŏ and Wa armies during the tenth year of the Yongnak era (400 A.D.). Moreover, Anra-jin, a name of a Wa collaborator, appears three times. These terms are closely related to Mimana Nihon Fu, and they are proper nouns well known to the Japanese from olden days. From this evidence, the inscription was thought to substantiate the existence of Mimana Nihon Fu.

Japanese read this to mean: "Paekche[21] and Silla had long been subject peoples of Koguryŏ and had originally presented tribute to Koguryŏ, but in 391 the Wa [Japan] came, crossing the sea, and made subjects of Paekche, _____, and Silla." Thus, on this basis the Japanese believed that Japan sent troops in 391, conquered Paekche and Silla, which had been dependencies of Koguryŏ, made them subject to Japan, and occupied the southern part of the Korean peninsula.

The first Korean reaction to this Japanese reading and interpretation came from Chŏng In-bo. According to Chŏng, the Japanese reading is correct in saying that Paekche and Silla presented tribute to Koguryŏ and were Koguryŏ subjects. But his reading differs from that point on. He divides the remaining part of that passage into four sections of seven, three, six, and four characters each. The first of these he reads, "The Wa invaded in 391"; the second, "[In response to the Wa invasion] Koguryŏ crossed the sea and defeated the Wa"; and the third, "[In the war between Koguryŏ and Japan] Paekche conspired with Japan and [verb] Silla." The verb is unclear, but Chŏng says it probably was "joined in the attack on. . . ." As for the last group of four characters, Chŏng says that they belong to the next sentence, which deals with the events of 396, and should read, "Because Paekche had originally been a subject of Koguryŏ. . . ."

This reading is based on an ingenious conception, and one can logically agree with it.[22] However, in this the subjects and objects of verbs shift too much. In classical Chinese one may omit subjects and objects, but this reading is extreme in this respect with the result that it is unnatural as classical Chinese. Also, if Koguryŏ had, in fact, crossed the sea and defeated Wa, as Chŏng maintains, then one would expect these meritorious deeds of King Kwanggaet'o to be spelled out more explicitly. Such vagueness is not in keeping with those passages on the stele that extol the victories of the king. One can only conclude that Chŏng In-bo's reading is farfetched.

Pak Si-hyŏng's reading is not substantially different from Chŏng's, and accordingly I shall omit an explanation of it.

---

21. The first two characters read here as "Paekche" were a pejorative for Paekche. All subsequent references to this term in this paper will use "Paekche."

22. Chŏng In-bo's argument is as follows. According to the Japanese reading, both Paekche and Silla were subjugated by Wa. If they had been subjects of Wa, this would have been an act of rebellion against Koguryŏ, and both Paekche and Silla would have been equally guilty. However, King Kwanggaet'o punished only Paekche, and this does not make sense. Furthermore, if Paekche was destroyed by Wa and became its subject, Paekche was the victim of aggression and Wa was the aggressor. It is unlike a king to leave the aggressor alone and attack the victim of the aggression. The king should have attacked the aggressor.

Kim Sŏk-hyŏng's reading and interpretation are rather different. The passage that Chŏng divided into four phrases Kim divides into two, breaking after the first seven characters. The first of these phrases he reads, "In 391 the Wa came and attacked." The second phrase is, "[In response to the Wa attack] Koguryŏ crossed the sea, defeated Paekche, [verb] Silla, and made them subject peoples." At first glance, it may seem queer for Koguryŏ to respond to a Wa invasion by attacking Paekche, but Kim's idea is that the Wa were not Japanese, but Koreans of Paekche descent who had settled in northern Kyūshū, establishing a Paekche colony. That was why it was necessary to attack the Wa homeland of Paekche to suppress the Wa.

Kim's reading has fewer unnatural elements than that of Chŏng Inbo. Nevertheless, one must accept as a premise that Wa was a Paekche colony for his interpretation to make sense, and that is just too complicated to be acceptable. Moreover, in the very next passage, the one dealing with 396, Koguryŏ again attacks Paekche. If King Kwanggaet'o had already defeated Paekche in 391, it does not make sense for him to attack again in 396. Even more problematical is the fact that passages in the inscription that describe military expeditions being with either chiao-ch'ien[a] or wang-kung-shuai[b]. Chiao-ch'ien is used in situations in which the king orders his subordinates out on an expedition, while wang-kung-shuai is used when the king leads the expedition in person. In the passage for 391, however, neither phrase appears. Moreover, each passage dealing with expeditions always and necessarily records a victorious outcome, but in 391 no victory was mentioned. For these reasons, therefore, I am unable to concur with Kim Sŏk-hyŏng's reading.

Aside from these, there are many other problems in the reading and interpretation of the inscription, but these, dealing with the year 391, are the most problematic. To read and interpret this passage correctly, one must study the logic behind the composition of the inscription.

### 4. The Logic of the Inscription and Its Reading

The stele was erected in the second year after the death of King Kwanggaet'o. At that time the memory of the king's deeds no doubt remained fresh in the minds of the Koguryŏ people. Consequently, it is probably safe to assume that the inscription reflected reality fairly accurately. However, the inscription was written to eulogize the king's distinguished service, and that meant one could expect some exaggeration or the presence of some elements that were not factual. One cannot accept the totality of the inscription as fact.

In studying the inscription, one must first of all follow the logic of the inscription itself, that is, one must put oneself in the place of the writer of the inscription in reading it and must come to understand the facts as expressed in it. Thereafter, one must determine the validity of those facts. One's study must be a two-stage process. First of all, let us consider the logic behind the composition of the inscription.

According to the inscription, Koguryŏ was originally suzerain of the entire Korean peninsula, and since ancient times both Paekche and Silla had been dependencies that would forever belong to Koguryŏ. Such was the fundamental position of the author of the inscription with respect to the international relations of the three Korean kingdoms.

There appeared, however, a force that upset these relations, and that was the invasion of the Wa in 391. The Wa drew Paekche into an alliance, attacked Silla, and was hostile to Koguryŏ. The Alla people were also mobilized at the time of the attack on Silla.

Whether Paekche had in fact originally been a Koguryŏ dependent, it did conspire with the Wa to resist Koguryŏ, and in alliance with the Wa attacked Silla. Paekche had violated the international order.

Silla fell before the onslaught of Paekche and the Wa. But that notwithstanding, it retained its loyal attitude toward Koguryŏ and requested Koguryŏ aid.

In these new circumstances, King Kwanggaet'o thoroughly punished the offenders and exerted his full effort to aid those who remained true. First of all, in 396 he punished the offending Paekche and defeated the Paekche king. In 399, Silla requested assistance, and in the next year, 400, he responded by dispatching a great army that defeated the Wa who had invaded Silla, and the Alla, whom the Wa had mobilized as allies. Again in 407, he administered a crushing defeat to the Wa who invaded Taebang. In this way, the offenders were all defeated by the military might of King Kwanggaet'o, and the radiance of his authority shone throughout the entire Korean peninsula.

Such was the thinking that lay behind the writing of the king's inscription. We must now reread the entry for 391 following this thinking:

(教遣) (王躬率)

百残新羅旧是属民由来朝貢
而倭以辛卯年来渡海破百残
羅以為臣民

What one must not forget in reading this passage is its placement in the text immediately preceding the passage for 396 that tells of the punitive expedition against Paekche. This sentence is an interpolation that aims to legitimate King Kwanggaet'o's suppression of Paekche. Now let us consider the sentence with that in mind.

The first phrase (from the beginning through tribute) I read as most others have before, that is, "Paekche and Silla had long been subject peoples of Koguryŏ and from the beginning presented tribute to Koguryŏ." This phrase reflects the fundamental position of the writer of the inscription, who believed that Koguryŏ had originally controlled Paekche and Silla.

Immediately following that phrase appears the term "Wa." And the Wa enter the scene as the agent that disrupts the three-kingdom international order in which Koguryŏ controls Paekche and Silla. Thus, we take as the next phrase the ten characters following (through destroy) and read it as, "Then the Wa in 391 came crossing the sea and destroyed. . . ." Since there is no object of the verb "destroy," it is unnatural to break there, but I interpret it to mean "to destroy the previously existing international order."[23]

Next come the last ten characters. The Wa have entered and upset the status quo. In these circumstances, Paekche conspires with Wa and becomes a traitor to Koguryŏ. This phrase shows that Paekche joined Wa in the attack on Silla. Thus, I read the last ten characters: "Paekche _____ Silla and made it a tributary." The blank is unclear, but it is a verb. If one reads it this way, then the following passage, dealing with the king's attack in 396 against Paekche, becomes understandable.

This is my reading of the sentence at issue, and this suits the logic of the inscription. Also, as a reading of classical Chinese, the subject is clear, and it is not unnatural.

There is, however, one problem. The text that I have used is the one that has long been widely known, and in it there is that last ten-character phrase with the two blank spaces. The two blanks are illegible and are presumed to be the result of damage. There are thought to have been characters in the blanks at the time the stele was made, but there remains the possibility that no characters were ever there. The reason for this doubt is that the surface of the stele is deeply concave where the two spaces are. It is not clear whether this concavity appeared later or whether it was there when the stele was erected. If, it appeared later, then there is no problem. But if the concavity were there at the outset, then it would have been impossible to carve characters in that space with the result that the two characters would never have existed.

---

23. The character "p'a" (to destroy) was illegible when the North Korean scholars studied the inscription in 1963. It might have originally been some character other than "p'a."

If this latter supposition is correct, then my reading will fail. In my reading, the space between Paekche and Silla must have contained characters, and there must have been a verb. If we presume that the two characters never existed, then we lost our verb and have two proper nouns, one immediately after the other, and Paekche, of course, ceases to be a subject. My reading would not stand.[24]

## 5. The Korean Peninsula in the Late Fourth and Early Fifth Centuries

Now that we have looked at the thinking that lay behind the writing of the stele inscription, let us examine the extent to which the stele reflects historical fact. For this purpose we need to depict the contemporary circumstances using the *Samguk sagi,* the oldest Korean history, and then to compare that with the description on the stele.[25]

According to the *Samguk sagi,* the most striking development in the Korean peninsula during the late fourth and early fifth centuries was the southern advance of Koguryŏ. Paekche and Silla displayed a complex reaction toward this advance.

Paekche resisted Koguryŏ, attacking the Koguryŏ city of P'yŏngyang in 371 and killing the Koguryŏ ruler, King Kogugwŏn, in battle. Thereafter, Paekche and Koguryŏ fought successive wars (in 386, 389, 390, 392, 393, 394, and 395) in the decade from 386 to 395. Again in 398 and 399 Paekche laid plans for a large-scale expedition against Koguryŏ. During the reign of King Kwanggaet'o (391–412), especially in the first half of the reign, severe wars continued between the two countries. For King Kwanggaet'o, Paekche was a formidable enemy.

Silla differed from Paekche in that it avoided military confrontation. The royal family sent hostages to Koguryŏ on two occasions, from 392 to 401 and again from 412 to 418. There was also one occasion in 417 when Koguryŏ sent troops to Kyŏngju, the Silla capital, and intervened in the royal succession. From the point of view of King Kwanggaet'o, Silla was submissive.

Thus, although both Paekche and Silla felt pressure from Koguryŏ, their respective responses were polar. At that point, relations between Paekche and Silla were shaken, too. At the end of the fourth century their relations were satisfactory, but just at century's end they worsened,

---

24. The two missing words are the most important part of this reexamination of the inscription.

25. To understand the relationship between ancient Japan and Korea, the *Nihon shoki* should be used in addition to the *Samguk sagi.* However, there are many problems with the *Nihon shoki,* and complicated problems are omitted here.

and in 403 Paekche invaded Silla. To meet the threat, Silla had no choice
but to rely on its ties to Koguryŏ.[26]

Next let us consider the relations of Wa with the three Korean kingdoms. The *Samguk sagi* says absolutely nothing about Koguryŏ's relations with Wa. The Wa, who appear as Koguryŏ enemies in the stele inscription several times, show up nowhere in the records relating to
Koguryŏ in the *Samguk sagi*. This is probably the fault of the *Samguk
sagi* rather than a reflection of a lack of relations in reality.

Most of the records of Paekche relations with Wa in the *Samguk
sagi* are concentrated in the period 397 to 428. Their relations were
friendly, and they exchanged embassies and gifts. Notably, in 397
Paekche's King Asin sent the crown prince, Chŏnji, to Wa as a hostage.
Chŏnji remained in Wa until 405, but hearing news of his father's death,
he returned home and assumed the throne himself. On the return journey, Wa soldiers accompanied Chŏnji as guards and assisted at the enthronement. The reason Paekche sent a hostage to Wa undoubtedly was
that it needed Wa assistance against the southward advance of Koguryŏ.

Wa relations with Silla are plentifully recorded in the *Samguk sagi*.
Some of these records show a peaceful relationship, but the vast majority
are records of Wa people invading Silla, as will be explained below.
These relations began very early, and in the period under consideration
Wa people raided Silla in 393, 405, 407, and 415. In 393, especially, Wa
people surrounded the capital at Kŭmsŏng (Kyŏngju) for five days. Not
only did Silla drive the invaders off, they also planned in 408 to attack
Wa bases in Tsushima.

In 402, while Silla was suffering these Wa invasions, the king,
Silsŏng, sent Misahŭn, son of the former king (Namul) to Wa as a hostage.[27] The probable reason was to stop the Wa invasions by showing
good faith to the Wa. But the plan did not work, as is evident from continued Wa raids thereafter. As previously explained, Silla also sent
hostages to Koguryŏ twice. And the fact that Silla sent hostages to both
countries suggests its painful position.

On the one hand, Silla hostages resided in Wa from 402 to 418, and

26. In 1946, a bronze vase was found during the excavation of the Hou tomb in Kyŏngju.
It had an inscription: "Ŭlmyonyŏn kukkangsan kwanggae t'oji hot'aewang hou." The
year Ŭlmyo was the third year after the death of King Kwanggaet'o (415 A.D.). This was a
vase in commemoration of King Kwanggaet'o, a relic signifying Koguryŏ's dominance over
Silla.

27. According to the *Samguk yusa,* Prince Mihae (also known as Mijilhŭi) was sent to
Wa as a hostage in 390 A.D. and returned in 425. Mihae was the same person as Misahŭn of
the *Samguk sagi*. The years of exit and reentry are different in the *Samguk sagi*. It is not
known which account is correct. The years given in the *Samguk sagi* are used here.

on the other, a Paekche hostage was there between 397 and 405, as previously mentioned. This meant that during the period 402–405 Wa held hostages from both Paekche and Silla simultaneously. That fact suggests that the kingdom of Wa held a position of considerable influence vis-a-vis both Paekche and Silla, and the Wa role in Korean history of the time cannot be ignored.

Up to this point I have outlined conditions in Korea during the late fourth and early fifth centuries based on the *Samguk sagi,* and these may be summarized as follows.

1. Koguryŏ was advancing southward and putting pressure on Paekche and Silla.
2. Paekche strongly resisted Koguryŏ throughout, while Silla submitted.
3. Paekche invaded Silla.
4. In the struggles among the three kingdoms the Wa intervened, aided Paekche, invaded Silla, and took hostages from both countries.

Now if we attempt to compare the *Samguk sagi* account with the King Kwanggaet'o inscription, we find several points of agreement. First, for Koguryŏ, Paekche was an enemy and Silla was an ally. Second, Paekche attacked Silla. Third, Wa allied with Paekche. However, the Koguryŏ-Wa relationship appears only on the stele and not in the *Samguk sagi.* As we have seen, that is probably a failing on the part of the *Samguk sagi.* On the other hand, the sending of Silla hostages to Wa and the negotiations with Wa are only in the *Samguk sagi* and not on the stele. That is an omission from the inscription.

Thus, the two accounts agree in broad outline and differ only in detail. Moreover, the differences are not contradictions; I believe the two sources complement one another.

Finally, let us look once again at the passage from the inscription that we examined earlier. The part that reads, "Paekche and Silla had long been subject peoples of Koguryŏ and originally presented tribute to Koguryŏ" states the legitimacy of Koguryŏ's control over Paekche and Silla. That, however, flies in the face of the facts. Paekche fought against Koguryŏ from the outset and continued its wars during the reign of King Kwanggaet'o. Silla did send hostages twice during the late fourth and early fifth centuries and showed a submissive attitude toward Koguryŏ, but that did not mean that Silla was a Koguryŏ dependency. Accordingly, the first part of the passage from the inscription is hyperbole, not fact.

The second part of the inscription says, "Then the Wa in 391 came crossing the sea and destroyed [the international order]." If one considers this in the context of the time, the Wa did invade Silla. In 393 the

Wa surrounded the Silla capital for five days, and in 402 they took hostages from Silla. At the time, that could only be construed as an invasion of Silla. This part of the passage, therefore, reflects the reality of the Wa invasion of Silla.

The last part, which says, "Paekche conspired with Wa, _____ Silla, and made it a tributary," is again hyperbole, not fact. In 397 Paekche did send hostages to Wa, and in 403 it did invade Silla, but it never made Silla into a tributary.

In this way, then, those parts of the inscription that are problematic are exaggerations and run counter to fact. The 391 passage as a whole is an interpolation that shows the writer's desire to legitimate King Kwanggaet'o's expedition against Paekche. It does not express a fact.

### 6. Who the Wa Were

The last major problem remaining is the identity of the Wa. According to the inscription on the stele, they conspired with Paekche, invaded Silla, and fought Koguryŏ. According to the *Samguk sagi,* they constantly invaded Silla, allied with Paekche, and took hostages from both. Who and what were these Wa?

Previously, most Japanese scholars thought of Wa as the Japanese state. If this interpretation is correct, then at the end of the fourth century and the beginning of the fifth century the Yamato state had unified the Japanese archipelago and had established a strong monarchy. But whether we really can regard the Wa as the Yamato state demands serious scrutiny.

I propose to consider the identity of the Wa by examining their characteristics as recorded in the "Annals of the Silla Court" (Silla pon'gi) taken from the *Samguk sagi.*

In the *Silla pon'gi,* which covers a period beginning in the mythical age before the Christian era down to A.D. 500,[28] the Wa appear forty-nine times. After analyzing these entries, I have found the following:

1. The country of Wa lay on the other side of the sea, and it had a king.

2. The Wa people constantly invaded Silla. Of the forty-nine entries, thirty-six concern invasions.

3. The Wa invasions were concentrated in the summer (months four, five, and six in the lunar calendar). Of the thirty-six invasions, twenty-three were in the summer. There were few in the spring (months

---

28. In the Silla *pon'gi* of the *Samguk sagi,* the term "Wa" appears continuously from the era before Christ to 500 A.D., but disappears for about a century and a half thereafter. It does not reappear until the second half of the seventh century. The absence of the term "Wa" from the account for more than a century and a half is a problem.

one, two, and three) and fall (months seven, eight, and nine), and there were none at all in the winter.[29]

4. At the beginning of the fifth century, as stated earlier, the Wa people's advance base was in Tsushima.

5. The Wa people at times formed into powerful forces that attacked the capital at Kŭmsŏng (Kyŏngju) and other cities. In most cases, however, they were small parties that attacked the seacoast.

6. Wa raiders seized people and property from Silla, but they never occupied any area continuously for a long period.

If one considers these factors, it is apparent that the Wa who raided Silla were pirates who crossed over seasonally, kidnapped people and stole property, and then returned. The country of Wa had a base on Tsushima and was a pirate kingdom that raided Silla.

Such, then, were the Wa who appear in the *Silla pon'gi*. Where the center of the Wa country was, the *Silla pon'gi* does not make clear. But the fact that the Wa were pirates who raided Silla on a seasonal basis is suggestive. It is unreasonable to believe that a pirate country would be in the Yamato area (in the modern Kinki area). It would be more natural for it to be along the coast near Korea. The most natural place for us to hypothesize would be northern Kyūshū.[30] In all probability the country of Wa had its main base in northern Kyūshū, had an advance base in Tsushima, and raided Silla seasonally.

I believe that the Wa of the King Kwanggaet'o stele were the same Wa that appear in the *Silla pon'gi* of the *Samguk sagi*. They were not the Yamato state, but a kingdom in northern Kyūshū.

At present, debate continues about the existence and character of the "Mimana Nihon Fu." The *Nihon shoki* says that it did exist. But it does not appear in Korean records. If the Mimana Nihon Fu had existed, there should be some relic or remains of it. To date no such site has emerged, and according to archeological findings, the Mimana Nihon Fu did not exist. We can only conclude that it was a creation of the *Nihon shoki*.

---

29. The Wa attacked more often during the summer because the sea was calm then. The Wa people did not have the ships and the navigational skills necessary to cross rough seas.

30. According to the accounts by Pak Che-sang (Kim Che-sang in the *Samguk yusa*), who was active in rescuing the hostages sent from Silla to Wa, Wa was not far from Silla, and its capital was said to have faced the sea. To view the Wa as the Yamato regime is thus contrary to the account of Pak Che-sang (Kim Che-sang).

# Military Revolt in Koryŏ: The 1170 Coup d'État

*Edward J. Shultz*
WEST OAHU COLLEGE

THE importance of the military has too often been ignored in Chinese and Korean history.[1] Chinese and Korean societies have emphasized the scholar, and they have prided themselves on seeking peaceful solutions to their problems. By nature traditional China and Korea were pacific, and only when their systems could not operate effectively from such a posture did they turn to military means for help. Yet rarely were military personnel allowed freedom from civilian restraints. Even in crises, the military remained subordinate to civilian rule. Often civilian leaders took charge of military preparations and assumed command on the battlefield. In Korea, civilian rule was the norm between the tenth and twentieth centuries. The only major exception occurred during one century, from 1170 to 1270, when military officers seized power and ruled the country.

Traditionally there has been a bias against this period of military rule in Korea. The Chinese Confucian classics were the ideological mainstay of the Korean political system, and they emphasized a philoso-

AUTHOR'S NOTE: I would like to acknowledge Hugh Kang, my former advisor at the University of Hawaii—Manoa, and Dan Boylan, my colleague at West Oahu College, for their many helpful suggestions.

1. Two exceptions are Frank A. Kierman, Jr., and John K. Fairbank, ed., *Chinese Ways in Warfare* (Cambridge: Harvard University Press, 1974) and Yi Kibaek, *Koryŏ pyŏngjesa yŏn'gu* (Seoul, 1968).

phy of civilian rule.[2] The Confucian scholars who compiled the dynastic records of the Koryŏ dynasty in the fifteenth century adhered to this view.[3] To them military rule, which commenced with a coup d'état in 1170, was unnatural, a sign that Koryŏ society was politically bankrupt, and the task was to discover how this had happened. The question was simple: What went wrong? They looked to King Ŭijong (1146–1170), whom the military deposed, and found him lacking moral character and misled by followers and eunuchs. The answer to their question, what went wrong, was also simple: Ŭijong, the king, was at fault. One historian commented:

> The essence of ruling the country lies in economizing and loving the people. Ŭijong built many ponds and pavilions through excessive expenditures and overworking the people. With his favorites he did nothing but sink into pleasure. Among his councilors of state and remonstrating officials, none could caution him. In the end, it brought his banishment to Kŏje island; this was fitting.[4]

But Ŭijong alone was not to be held totally responsible. The men Ŭijong chose to attend him were also responsible for the coup d'état of 1170. Again a historian commented:

> If Ŭijong had sincerely sought loyal and honest people, then definitely his government would have been good and praised by later generations. Unfortunately the people he listened to were flatterers and manipulators. In appointing officials they stressed drinking and poetry and neglected political discussion.[5]

The king not only neglected his duties, but placed too much emphasis on such non-Confucian activities as Buddhist practices and various superstitions. This attitude, according to traditional interpretations, was equally corrupting and certainly contributed to his demise.

2. John K. Fairbank, "Introduction: Varieties of the Chinese Military Experience" in *Chinese Ways in Warfare*, p. 7, states:

> This disesteem of physical coercion was deeply imbedded in the Confucian teaching. The superior man *(chün-tzu)*, extolled in the classics as the highest product of self-cultivation, should be able to attain his ends without violence. This was because of the optimistic belief that virtuous and proper conduct exerted such an edifying attraction upon the beholder that he accorded moral prestige to the actor. Right conduct thus gave one moral authority, a kind of power. To do the right thing in the right way and at the proper time not only maintained the web of civilized relationships; it also confirmed one's position within it.

3. The two dynastic histories of the Koryŏ dynasty are the *Koryŏsa* (Yŏnse edition; Seoul, 1972), hereafter cited as *KS;* and the *Koryŏsa chŏryo* (Hōsa Bunkō edition; Tokyo, 1960), hereafter cited as *KSC*.

4. *KSC,* 11:42a.

5. Ibid., 11:54a–b.

Now the former king [Ŭijong] emphasized Buddhist laws and reverently respected shamanistic gods. He established sutras and solemn masses, prayers for favors, wine feasts, and costly services. He conscripted funds without moderation. Everywhere he served Buddha and the gods. Flatterers . . . were at his side, crafty people . . . were his close eunuchs, treacherous people . . . became his diviners, and his favorite concubine, Mubi, took charge of the palace. They led the king's mind with their wishes; they flattered each other; clever words prevailed as remonstrance retreated.[6]

To the Confucian scholar the picture was clear. Ŭijong was weak. He lived in ostentation, followed dubious religious beliefs, and accepted harmful advice. He failed to heed thoughtful and worthy words of caution. Furthermore, his deportment brought on resentment between the military and civilian elements in his government, which, according to these historians, resulted in the massacre of all civilians in the country with the revolt in 1170.

This interpretation of the military coup rested unchallenged until the middle of the present century when contemporary scholars started probing into Korea's history, seeking to reinterpret the past. Yi Pyŏngdo led in the reevaluation of the period, but, swayed by the evidence that the traditional historians presented, he focused on Ŭijong's neglect of state affairs. Yi accepted the interpretation that Ŭijong was hopelessly lost in his love of luxury and was captivated by charlatans who offered him worthless panaceas as solutions to his problems.[7]

At the same time, Kim Sanggi was presenting his own interpretation of the period, and in assessing the causes of the 1170 coup d'état, he concluded that civilian maltreatment of the military was a major factor in the military revolt. Kim, by recounting the petty harassments and punishments suffered by the military officers, demonstrated how the officers had no recourse but a coup d'état to redress genuine grievances.[8] To many scholars it became apparent that the military officers were indeed neglected and bullied as the dynasty progressed. In studying Koryŏ military institutions, Yi Kibaek essentially concurred with this interpretation, especially when considering the duties that military personnel performed. In explaining the revolt, Yi points to:

6. *KS,* 19:10a–11a; *KSC,* 11:59a–60a.

7. See Yi Pyŏngdo, *Koryŏ sidae ŭi yŏn'gu* (Seoul, 1954), pp. 234–241, and *Han'guksa: chungsep'yŏn* (Seoul, 1961), pp. 452–458.

8. See Kim Sanggi, *Koryŏ sidaesa* (Seoul, 1961), pp. 413–417. Kim's thesis is essentially reiterated by Min Pyŏngha, "Ch'oe ssi chŏnggwŏn ŭi chibae kigu," *Han'guksa,* vol. 7 (Seoul: Kuksa P'yŏnch'an Wiwŏnhoe, 1973), pp. 86–90. Min asserts that the military revolt evolved out of contradictions in Koryŏ's aristocratic society that led to discontent among military personnel.

the intensive complaints of the central army soldiers, who were experiencing economic and social decline. More often than not they were mobilized for corvée labor, thereby demonstrating the changing character of their service from military to labor. In addition, military land was improperly allotted, thus depriving poverty-stricken soldiers of the capacity for military service.[9]

Writing in the early 1960s, Pyŏn T'aesŏp offered a different interpretation. Pyŏn asserted that the military coup was not caused by a decline in the social status of the military. Quite the opposite was the case. Life was improving, according to Pyŏn, and with rising expectations, military personnel sought still better conditions through a coup d'état.[10]

This study specifically reassesses these interpretations by examining Ŭijong's reign and the military revolt of 1170 in terms of the political realities and conflicts of the age. The thesis here is that the revolt, above all else, was a result of power struggles in the dynasty. There is evidence of conflict in earlier reigns, but it is not until Ŭijong's rule that the civilian elite lost control of the situation. There was a long, constant sparring for power between two basic groups: the king and his followers on one side and the central aristocratic clans on the other. The prize was absolute authority over Korea. The participants in these two groups, however, were not fixed. And to add to the complexity of the struggle there was disunity within each group. Often the royal family was divided among itself, and occasionally the aristocrats split into factions. Dynastic institutions often became embroiled in these disputes too. In Ŭijong's reign, for example, it is apparent that the censorial organs (the Ŏsadae and Sŏngnang, collectively known as the Taegan) at times became the focus of conflict.

During Ŭijong's reign, military personnel emerged as arbiters of these issues. The military had the means to resolve the disputes, and it also had a vested interest in reforming a system that daily became more ineffective. Military officers quickly evolved from arbiters into dynastic rulers.

An analysis of the 1170 purge confirms these basic themes. The new policy makers immediately exiled King Ŭijong and many of his closest associates, including a number of aristocrats. The military officers who settled the struggle became firmly entrenched, and civilian aristocrats who played a crucial role in the revolt continued to share governmental

9. Yi Kibaek, "Korea—The Military Tradition," *Traditional Culture and Society of Korea: Thought and Institutions,* ed. Hugh H. W. Kang (Honolulu: Center for Korean Studies, 1975), p. 21. See also, Yi Kibaek, *Koryŏ pyŏngjesa yŏn'gu,* pp. 141, 289.

10. P'yŏn T'aesŏp, "Koryŏ muban yŏn'gu," in *Koryŏ chŏngch'i chedosa yŏn'gu* (Seoul, 1971), pp. 342–398. This article appeared earlier in *Asea yŏn'gu,* 8, no. 3 (March 1965).

power with the military for the next century. Royal power, on the other hand, barely survived.

### Kingship in Middle Koryŏ

Kings in Korea have rarely fared well. The king as a Confucian leader had vast potential in exercising his authority, yet in practice he knew only constraints. The Koryŏ dynasty had few strong monarchs; nearly all were emasculated by powerful aristocrats and dynastic institutions. As one scholar stated:

Korean kings suffered from four major types of problems. Their traditional legitimacy was relatively weak; they were engaged with the bureaucracy and the aristocracy in competition for political power; they had to compete with the landowning and privileged aristocracy for control over economic and man-power resources; and they were hamstrung by the normative constraints of Neo-Confucian thought.[11]

In the Koryŏ dynasty the domination of the aristocrats challenged all kings and was the major reason for a weak monarchy.[12]

The twelfth century, however, began in Korea with the throne making limited attempts to reassert its authority. Both Sukchong (1095–1105) and Yejong (1105–1122) sought to expand their power[13] and bring changes to the power structure. They emphasized the state examination system *(kwagŏ)*, recruiting occasionally up to thirty-five men into the state administration at one sitting.[14] During Yejong's reign a major change to the regional system occurred with the establishment of district offices *(kammugwan)* throughout the country.[15] The central government appointed and sent officials, through the district offices, to the rural areas and was thus able to exercise more direct authority over the various regions. This curbed the power of influential regional leaders like the township headmen *(hojang)* and gave more authority to the central

11. James B. Palais, "Political Leadership in the Yi Dynasty," *Political Leadership in Korea,* ed. Dae-Sook Suh and Chae-jin Lee (Seattle: University of Washington Press, 1976), p. 4. This description of Yi Chosŏn monarchs is also appropriate for Koryŏ kings, with the exception of the term Neo-Confucianism, which became important only with Yi Chosŏn, although Confucian ideology in general restrained Koryŏ kings.

12. Hugh H. W. Kang, "The Development of the Korean Ruling Class from Late Silla to Early Koryŏ" (Ph.D. diss., University of Washington, 1964), p. 298.

13. Kim Yun'gon, "Koryŏ kwijok sahoe ŭi che mosun," in *Han'guksa,* vol. 7, p. 43, asserts this thesis, but marshals insufficient evidence to support his contention that they succeeded in this endeavor.

14. Hŏ Hungsik, "Koryŏ ŭi kukchagam si wa irul t'onghan sinbun yudong," *Han'guksa yŏn'gu,* no. 12 (1976):53–90, suggests that the leading aristocratic clans were consciously doing this, making a sham of the examinations by passing many close relatives and family members. He does not explain, however, whether the king acquiesced in this out of the hope for more support of his own position.

15. *KS,* 77:43a.

government.[16] The king and the aristocrats alike generally supported changes, because they hoped to use them to expand their authority and influence.

Sukchong almost succeeded in freeing himself from the domination of the aristocracy. He came to the throne just after the powerful aristocratic Kyŏngwŏn Yi clan had been subjugated by a combined force of central aristocrats and military personnel. The new king, hopeful of benefiting from the struggles among the central aristocrats, sought to assert his own authority. Unlike his predecessors and his successor, who married Kyŏngwŏn Yi clan members, Sukchong avoided such a restricting marriage alliance by choosing instead a member of the Chŏngju Yu clan.

The royal family intended to reestablish the independence of the throne, a stance becoming even more apparent when Yejong died late in 1122. At that time there was an internal struggle as two brothers of the deceased king plotted to prevent the succession of a monarch who was partial to the Kyŏngwŏn Yi clan.[17] Their ploy failed, and the Kyŏngwŏn Yi clan recouped much of its former authority.

Under Injong (1122–1146) monarchical independence diminished. Yi Chagyŏm, a Kyŏngwŏn Yi and grandfather of the young king, dominated the early part of the reign and dictated court policy.[18] After a combined aristocratic and military force removed Yi Chagyŏm, Injong faced another challenge from the monk Myoch'ŏng.[19] Again the king succeeded in meeting this threat through the combined efforts of the central aristocrats and military personnel. In the last half of Injong's reign, two aristocratic families, the Kyŏngju Kim clan and the Chŏngan Im clan, emerged to leadership.

The Kyŏngju Kim clan actually had been a prominent family throughout the dynasty. As direct descendants of the last Silla king, Kim Pu, Kyŏngju Kim clansmen actively participated in the early Koryŏ dynasty.[20] In the eleventh century they achieved new prominence when four members of one generation successfully completed the state examination and entered government service.[21] They served in Injong's administra-

---

16. Some scholars have asserted that a new group of regional bureaucrats was entering the central administration from this time and clashed with the central aristocratic clans for dynastic leadership. See, for example, Kim Yun'gon, "Koryŏ kwijok sahoe ŭi che mosun."

17. Two of Yejong's brothers, Taebaggong P'o and Taeyugong Ho, plotted with Han Anin and others to prevent Injong (1122–1146), who was the Kyŏngwŏn Yi clan's choice, from taking the throne. They failed and Yi Chagyŏm exiled the royal brothers. See Kang, "The Development of the Korean Ruling Class," p. 280.

18. Ibid., pp. 280–289.

19. Myoch'ŏng sought to establish a new dynasty with its capital in P'yŏngyang.

20. KSC, 3:48b.

21. Four sons of Kim Kun passed the examination: Puil, Puch'ŏl, Pup'il, and Pusik.

tion, aiding in both the ouster of Yi Chagyŏm and the pacification of Myoch'ŏng's revolt. The Chŏngan Im clan was equally important. Injong's wife was a member of this clan, and the three succeeding kings were her sons. The clan first achieved renown when one Im Ŭi successfully completed the state examination in 1070.[22] Three of his sons, Wŏnae, Wŏnjun, and Wŏnsuk, all reached high dynastic ranks. Yi Chagyŏm once banished Wŏnjun; however, after Yi himself was removed, the clan secured high and powerful government ranks.

### Ŭijong

Ŭijong, coming to the throne in 1146, quickly became embroiled in power struggles as, under his leadership, the court again made numerous ploys to assert its authority over the aristocrats. Yet his position was weak because of internal divisions within his own court. Ŭijong was challenged even before he came to the throne by his own immediate family's disapproval of his succession. Both his father, King Injong, and his mother, Lady Im, questioned his ability to rule. Injong had serious misgivings about Ŭijong's talent, and Lady Im, who was even more outspoken, openly favored her second son, Prince Kyŏng. Ŭijong won the throne only through the staunch support of the royal tutor Chŏng Sŭpmyŏng, who assured the royal parents that he would personally guide and instruct Ŭijong once the young man became king.[23] Succeeding to the throne with this cloud of opposition, Ŭijong found his effectiveness as a monarch and ability to exercise royal prerogatives curtailed. He realized that he would have to resort to forceful action if he wished to assert his authority. This need for independence ultimately would be fatal to his rule. It would cause him to accept uncritically support from any group, ultimately embroiling him in the internal power struggles of the central aristocrats.

Ŭijong, enthroned at the age of nineteen, was a talented, gifted young man with a keen appreciation for nature. Throughout his reign he wrote poetry on such diverse topics as the beauty of a rain shower and exotic flowers.[24] He also assembled the scholars of the day and judged their poetry, rewarding those who excelled.[25] Ŭijong enjoyed nature and sought to surround himself with its beauty. Under his guidance the palace grounds were landscaped, and many gardens and artificial ponds

22. Yi Nanyŏng, *Han'guk kŭmsŏngmun ch'ubo* (Seoul, 1968), p. 90.

23. *KS,* 98:23a; *KSC,* 11:8a.

24. *KS,* 18:16a, 19:7b–8a; *KSC,* 11:29b, 11:50a. On other occasions he summoned monks and wrote poetry in the moonlight. *KS,* 18:28b; *KS,* 11:39b. Or he recorded poems that came to him in a dream. *KS,* 18:35a–b; *KSC,* 11:44b.

25. *KS,* 17:34a, 18:2b; *KSC,* 11:11b–12a, 11:15b.

were constructed. The king entertained in pavilions roofed with porcelain and held sumptuous banquets and exotic performances there.[26] He also built gardens in the countryside. Once, hearing of an area where stream water collected, causing a dense growth of trees, Ŭijong ordered that a pavilion be constructed and rare plants and trees be brought there. Since the water was not deep enough for boats, a dam was also made to form a lake.[27] On another occasion townsmen, seeing a light moving through the trees behind the palace, were alarmed until they discovered it was only the king enjoying an evening stroll.[28] The king was an ardent traveler, as much at home in the countryside as in his capital, Kaegyŏng.[29]

Traditional historians have readily condemned these activities as frivolous and evidence of Ŭijong's inabilities as a monarch. What should not be ignored, however, is Ŭijong's aesthetic nature and remarkable taste for beauty. Neither should the political implications be disregarded. Ŭijong discovered that in turning to nature he was able to ignore the intense political feuding that was erupting in his court. He also realized that by bringing dissidents to his gardens, away from the turmoil of court politics, he might be able to reason with opponents and win them to his point of view. Ŭijong often did just this.

Ŭijong was also a devout Buddhist. Buddhist practices were in vogue at this time, and his reign witnessed repeated expressions of his religious fervor. On many of his excursions to the countryside, temples were the prime destinations. Here he prayed, meditated, and observed religious ceremonies.[30] While at home in the palace, Ŭijong also comforted himself by studying sutras and attending Buddhist masses.[31] The king actively repaired and constructed temples.[32] Furthermore, he was generous with the clergy and faithful alike. Ŭijong, as was customary with many kings, held maigre feasts for as many as thirty thousand monks.[33] Once

26. One popular activity was viewing beautiful flowers. *KS,* 18:5b; *KSC,* 11:19a. In addition to making the palace grounds as beautiful as possible, Ŭijong also collected rare animals and exotic birds. *KS,* 18:34a–35b; *KSC,* 11:29a. See also, *KS,* 18:15b, 18:17b–18a; *KSC,* 11:29b, 11:22b–23a.

27. *KS,* 18:33b–34a; *KSC,* 11:43a–b.

28. *KSC,* 11:13b.

29. *KS,* 17:36b–37a; *KSC,* 11:13a, 11:49a. Looking at 1163 specifically, Ŭijong left the capital much of the time.

30. *KS,* 17:21a, 18:8b, 18:9a; *KSC,* 11:1a, 11:23a, 11:23b.

31. Shortly after coming to the throne, he held prayers in Yongt'ongsa temple and read the Hwaŏm (Hwayen) scriptures for more than fifty days. *KS,* 17:21a; *KSC,* 11:1a.

32. In 1156 Ŭijong and his queen vowed that if a son were born to them they would make four sets of the Hwaŏm scriptures in gold and silver characters. When a son was born they repaired the walls at Hŭngwangsa temple and stored two copies there. *KS,* 18:5a–b; *KSC,* 11:18a–b. Earlier in 1154 Ŭijong constructed Chunghŭngsa temple in Sŏgyŏng. *KS,* 11:3a; *KSC,* 11:16a.

33. See, for example, *KS,* 18:3a; *KSC,* 11:16a.

on the road to Hŭngwangsa, Ŭijong saw an old woman and gave her cloth and wine.[34] The king undoubtedly turned to Buddhism because it provided solace and guidance in his daily life. This religion also offered religious solutions to problems besetting the kingdom.[35] By propitiating the deities and spirits a crisis could be settled, and by prayer and meditation a resolution to vexing conflicts could be found. In spite of the criticism of latter-day Confucian scholars, it was natural and proper for Ŭijong to have a close affiliation with Buddhism. It was a custom that had commenced with the start of the dynasty.

Confucian practices were not neglected by the king either. From his youth the king had been instructed in Confucian principles and was expected to use Confucian doctrine as a guide to behavior. In ruling, he often exhorted his officials and subjects to heed Confucian ideals and for himself sought to rectify wrongs. In 1160, in a strong Confucian tone, he decreed:

A king's virtue rests in seeking life, and despising death, and diligently relieving the people's agony. Recently the prisons have been full and the people are increasingly bothered by affairs. I am concerned with this. I will pardon individuals with the death penalty and lesser punishments, remit taxes for the rural regions, and distribute grain from the storehouses to aid the poor and destitute. The descendants of T'aejo who have not received their salaries and positions will be compensated. And I will command my officials to select, appoint, and recommend the pure and principled.[36]

When faced with a natural catastrophe, he searched for able and loyal officials.[37] And to demonstrate his concern for all subjects, he pardoned criminals and rewarded chaste widows, filial sons, and orphaned children.[38] Through each of these acts, Ŭijong was paying attention to necessary, symbolic acts, which in theory demonstrated his inherent ability as a Confucian monarch.

### Opposition to Ŭijong

Ŭijong's character and behavior can be understood more clearly by considering the problems confronting this young monarch. In his zeal to become an independent ruler he confronted opposition from his own

34. *KS*, 18:14a; *KSC*, 11:29a. On another trip to Pohyŏnwŏn, he gave a beggar cloth and then presented other travelers with enough rice and soup to last for two days. *KS*, 18:15b; *KSC*, 11:19b.

35. For example, on one occasion Ŭijong, warned of an evil omen, called for prayers to Buddhist images and held prayers in shrines throughout the country. *KSC*, 11:20a.

36. *KS*, 18:18b–19a; *KSC*, 11:31a–b. On other occasions the king also presented similar statements revealing a concern for the poor and the general welfare of his people. *KS*, 18:24a, 19:4a–5a; *KSC*, 11:36a, 11:47a–b.

37. *KS*, 17:37a; *KSC*, 11:13b.

38. *KS*, 17:22b, 18:11a; *KSC*, 11:2a, 11:25b. On some occasions he gave special grants to virtuous officials. *KS*, 18:21b; *KSC*, 11:33b.

family and from entrenched aristocrats. Aware of his parents' reluctance to endorse him as the monarch, Ŭijong quickly became suspicious of his brothers and his mother's clan, the Chŏngan Ims. One brother abandoned all political designs and became a monk at one of the major Buddhist temples, Hŭngwangsa.[39] Then in 1151 conflicts erupted into a large-scale purge when Ŭijong demoted Chŏng Sŏ, office chief of palace attendants *(naesi nangjung);* Ch'oe Yuch'ŏng, a councilor of state *(chaesang)* and former censor; and Yi Chaksŭng, a censor of miscellaneous affairs *(ŏsajapdan).* At the same time, he stripped his brother, Prince Kyŏng, of a number of titles.

Kyŏng was on good terms with his mother's family and especially with Im Kŭkchŏng. Through the Im clan, he was indirectly related to Chŏng Sŏ, Ch'oe Yuch'ŏng, and Yi Chaksŭng.[40] The king suspected a plot among Kyŏng and some of his distant relatives. Prompted by these doubts, a number of the king's attendants, led by a certain eunuch, Chŏng Ham, brought charges that Kyŏng had designs on the throne. Although the charges were not substantiated, Chŏng Ham concocted rumors about the relations between Prince Kyŏng and the extended maternal royal family. Kim Chonjung, an ally of the king, reinforced these tales. The histories indicate that his motives were far from pure: "Chonjung was on unfriendly terms with the queen's sister's husband, Office Chief of Palace Attendants Chŏng Sŏ, and the queen's brother, Transmitter *(sŏnsŭng)* Im Kŭkchŏng."[41] Kim also had an old friendship with the eunuch Chŏng Ham, and now because of petty grudges, he charged the atmosphere by playing on the king's own fears, culminating in the dismissal of these "anti-Ŭijong" officials.

The men demoted at this time not only shared a common bond through marriage ties, but had similar regional origins, as well.[42] Chŏng Sŏ, for example, was from Tongnae, near modern Pusan, and entered the dynastic service through a protective appointment *(ŭm),* being appointed a palace attendant *(naesi).*[43] The Chŏng family had long been prominent in local politics with many of its members acting as area township headmen *(hojang).* While a palace attendant, Sŏ probably first challenged the eunuchs and Kim Chonjung, and this might have contrib-

---

39. *KSC,* 11:17b.

40. Im Kŭkchŏng was Prince Kyŏng's maternal uncle. One of Im's sisters was married to Chŏng Sŏ. Chŏng Sŏ was the key man in extending these relations, for his sisters in turn married Ch'oe Yuch'ŏng and Yi Chaksŭng.

41. *KS,* 90:28a–29b; *KSC,* 11:9b–11a.

42. There is also minor evidence that might link this group with the excessive remonstrance of the censorial organs. Ch'oe Yuch'ŏng and Yi Chaksŭng were both members of the censorate and could have orchestrated much of the opposition to Ŭijong.

43. Yi Nanyong, *Han'guk kŭmsŏngmun ch'ubo,* p. 100.

uted to his demise. But other than his opposition to Chonjung and his close ties with Kyŏng, we know little at this time. One cannot help but wonder, however, whether Sŏ's own family background, as the grandson of a township headman, and his links with men of similar origins, like the Chŏngan Im and Tongju Ch'oe clans, might have been an additional factor in his banishment.[44] Opposition to Ŭijong was forming around such men as Chŏng Sŏ, Ch'oe Yuch'ŏng, and Im clansmen who were all from families with strong regional ties, relatively new to dynastic politics, and related to one another through marriage. One month after Sŏ was removed, his alleged crimes were recorded in the government register along with those of Ch'oe Yuch'ŏng and Yi Chaksŭng.

For the next five years little was heard from Chŏng Sŏ, Prince Kyŏng, or their relatives until suddenly in 1157 Ŭijong exiled Kyŏng to Ch'ŏnanbu and demoted Ch'oe Yuch'ŏng, Im Kŭkchŏng, Kim Iyŏng, Yi Chaksŭng, and Chŏng Sŏ. Kim Iyŏng was one of Sŏ's in-laws who had survived the earlier purge. This new incident was sparked by Ŭijong's suspicions that his mother's family still harbored ill will toward him. Fearing that his mother would in fact undo his plan, Ŭijong had sent her to Pojesa temple first and made it appear that he had no control over the ensuing events.[45] To Ŭijong, all of these people posed a threat to his power structure that could best be handled by dismissal or banishment. One historian concluded:

Prince Kyŏng's treason is not clear. His mother is still alive and suffers because of her son's exile. Ŭijong is ungrateful. Yuch'ŏng is upright and a renowned official of his age. Chaksŭng, pure, principled, and in every way a good censor, is disliked by Chŏng Ham and is unable to escape exile—alas![46]

Clearly fissures within the royal family were present, forcing the king to resort to drastic action to maintain his position.

Most of this purged group did not reappear until after the military coup of 1170. Still, even though Ŭijong removed them from the power structure, their interest in politics continued. This particular group had tenuous and somewhat indirect ties with the military. Kim Iyŏng, Chŏng Sŏ's brother-in-law, was related by marriage to Chŏng Chungbu, a leading general of the period who was instrumental in planning the 1170

---

44. The Im clan grew prominent in Injong's reign when individuals from many local clans were entering the central bureaucracy. Im Kŭkchŏng was married to a T'anju Han. This clan suffered under Yi Chagyŏm's earlier rebellion. Ch'oe Yuch'ŏng, another associate, was from the Tongju Ch'oe clan, and this family seems to have maintained itself as a prominent local family in Tongju since early in the dynasty. The lineage of Yi Chaksŭng remains obscure.

45. *KSC*, 11:21b–22a.

46. Ibid., 11:22a.

coup. Chungbu's son Kyun married Kim Iyŏng's daughter.[47] Other ties
between this group and the military are also apparent. Ch'oe Yuch'ŏng's
sons, In and Tang, both were registrars in the capital armies.[48] Although
these positions were civil posts, it might be inferred that through these
two men, both of whom became quite important after the 1170 coup, the
military leaders and this disgruntled group of officials might have been
able to communicate and share their distress over court politics.

If the royal maternal family and its supporters were one impediment
to the assertion of Ŭijong's authority, the aristocracy as a group also often sought to curtail monarchical power. As already indicated, historians
of the Koryŏ dynasty are nearly unanimous in concluding that Koryŏ
kingship was relatively weak compared to the vast power of the central
aristocratic clans. The locus of aristocratic political power was in a group
of officials collectively and individually called *chaesang* (councilors of
state).[49] Through group decisions, the councilors of state effectively
ruled the country, and in their united efforts, and often even singly, they
could impede independent royal action. The councilors of state were divided over Ŭijong, but another institution that became increasingly vocal
during the middle of the dynasty was the censorial organ, the Taegan.[50]
During the twelfth century, the Taegan launched numerous efforts in remonstrance and became an effective vehicle of opposition to court activities.

In Ŭijong's reign there was a vociferous barrage of criticism, nearly
constant in its condemnation, leveled against the king and his activities.
Institutionally, the censorial units had reached their maturity and were
exercising all the power they could muster to enforce their will. The censorate criticized Ŭijong in statement after statement attacking his poor
administration, his reckless appointments, and his general deportment.
No monarch was a paragon of virtue, least of all Ŭijong. Nevertheless,
the censors of this age were exercising remonstrance in the extreme, and
very quickly much of their criticism was in danger of losing its effectiveness.[51]

47. *KS,* 128:10a.
48. Yi Nanyong, *Han'guk kŭmsŏngmun ch'ubo,* p. 159.
49. For a more complete discussion of the councilors of state and aristocratic power in
general, see Edward J. Shultz, "Institutional Developments in Korea under the Ch'oe
House: 1196–1258" (Ph.D. diss., University of Hawaii, 1976), pp. 15–20, and Kang, "The
Development of the Korean Ruling Class."
50. For additional information on the censorial organs, see Park Yongwoon (Pak
Yongun), "Koryŏjo ŭi taegan chedo," *Yŏksa hakpo,* no. 52 (December 1971):1–54.
51. During Ŭijong's twenty-four-year reign, the censorate launched more than twenty-
five major protests. At least seventeen of these occurred within the first seven years of the
reign.

The censorate challenged general state affairs.[52] It also attacked repeatedly the king's enjoyment of polo *(kyŏkku)*, making it a cause célèbre until the king finally acquiesced and abandoned the game in 1152.[53] The men Ŭijong had recruited were equally suspect and unacceptable to the censors. They condemned the behavior of high-ranking officials who supported Ŭijong as well as eunuchs and palace attendants.[54] Chŏng Ham, the eunuch who had become influential through Ŭijong's favors, was a special target of repeated attacks.[55]

Ŭijong resisted these attacks in many different ways. One tactic was simply to ignore the protest.[56] When Ŭijong felt strongly about certain points he would pit his will against that of the censors, forcing them to accept his decisions.[57] On one occasion, Ŭijong was so incensed over the effrontery of a memorial that he burned it before the censor's eyes.[58] But this was extreme action, and Ŭijong preferred to employ diplomatic techniques. He repeatedly made overtures to leading officials and censors, inviting them to royal banquets and garden parties, and through the tested technique of wining and dining, he was able to realize many victories.[59] Ŭijong demonstrated considerable ingenuity in staving off censo-

52. See, for example, *KS,* 99:13a, 17:29a, 18:1b; *KSC,* 11:5a, 11:5b, 11:15a, 11:16b.

53. *KS,* 17:21a-b, 17:35b-36a; *KSC,* 17:1a-b, 11:14a. Other kings had enjoyed this sport, but none was criticized as much as Ŭijong for watching it.

54. See, for example, *KS,* 17:24a-b, 122:14a, 96:33a; *KSC,* 11:2b-3a, 11:30b, 11:31b-32a.

55. *KS,* 122:11a-12a; *KSC,* 11:9b-10a. Other protests occurred in 1152 and 1157. In 1158 the censorate made a dramatic stand against permitting Chŏng Ham to hold high government positions, saying, "Chŏng Ham's ancestor was unsubject-like and rebellious in T'aejo's reign and thus punished and made into a slave to keep him out of court. Now Ham advances and descendants of T'aejo's merit subjects will be forced to heed a traitorous person. We request that Ham's position be abolished and all those who conspire with him be made commoners." *KS,* 99:13b-14b, 122:13a-b; *KSC,* 11:26a-b.

56. *KS,* 17:23a, 18:25a; *KSC,* 11:2b, 11:37a. In 1151 when the censorate refused to recant, Ŭijong simply ignored it and went to watch polo. *KS,* 17:35b; *KSC,* 11:12a-b.

57. In 1151 he demoted one Yun Ŏnmun and four men who refused to recant. *KS,* 99:13a-b; *KSC,* 11:13b-14a. And in 1157, when an official refused to approve Chŏng Ham's appointment, Ŭijong exclaimed, "Nobles, you do not listen to my wishes. I eat, but have no taste, and sleep, but have no peace." On hearing this, the officials had no choice but comply with his demands. *KSC,* 11:24b-25a; *KS,* 122:12b. Although he won this round, the historians claim that as the eunuch's "power grew, wisdom was blocked. The *chaesang* and *taegan* were threatened and afraid. The officials closed their eyes and did not speak. In the end came Chŏng Chungbu's revolt. Alas!" *KS,* 122:13b; *KSC,* 11:25a. See also, *KS,* 96:33a; *KSC,* 11:31b-32a.

58. In 1163 the censorate, under the leadership of Mun Kŭkkyŏm, chided the king for supporting eunuchs and confidants who only damaged the throne. When Mun referred to scandals in the palace, Ŭijong, in anger, burned the petition and banished Mun. *KS,* 99:18a-b; *KSC,* 11:34a-b.

59. See, for example, *KS,* 18:5b-6a, 19:7a-b; *KSC,* 11:19a-b, 11:49b. In 1168, 1169, and 1170, Ŭijong held more than twenty parties, banquets, and cruises for the leading officials of the kingdom, often including members of the censorial organs.

rial criticism. Once in 1160 when all other measures seem to have failed him, he devised a unique way to silence his critics. The histories relate:

The king went to Injijae, also known as Kyŏngnyonjae. He presented a poem that read, "In a dream I heard of a truly happy place—the hermitage under Puso mountain." Accordingly the king had pavilions built there and decorated them. Daily with palace favorites he got drunk and enjoyed himself and had no concern for state affairs. The censorate requested him to desist, but the king, using his poem, would immediately explain the meaning of his dream to refute them. After this the censors could only stop.[60]

Ŭijong was learning many lessons in political strategy, and he was often successful. Sometimes he was even able to have the Taegan do his own bidding. No incident demonstrates this better than Ŭijong's successful use of the censorate to remove his major rivals in the royal maternal family in 1151 and then in 1157. On both occasions the king, confident of victory, called upon the censorate to investigate charges and won verdicts against his opponents.

### Ŭijong and His Supporters

To control the dynasty effectively, Ŭijong needed support. Denied or skeptical of the allegiance of his mother's family, the Chŏngan Im clan, and harried by a barrage of criticism from the censorate, Ŭijong looked to other sources for allies. This desire and need to have partisans ultimately led Ŭijong into great difficulties. It estranged him from certain groups who were instrumental in formulating dynastic policy, and it caused him to accept as allies people of dubious integrity, people who were frequently after the riches that royal association so easily brought.

Eunuchs have always been a traditional source of power for monarchs, and to the Confucian historians, the eunuchs who flourished under Ŭijong became his nemesis. Ŭijong looked to these people, however, because they were available and willing to aid him. They played prominent roles as royal advisers. Chŏng Ham, Ŭijong's favorite eunuch, was so powerful that he decided the fate of many civil and military officials. Other men, such as Kim Yu, by bribing eunuchs received sought-after appointments.[61] Eunuchs, accompanying the king on his travels, supervised royal expenses and used many such opportunities to enrich themselves. They also conspired with monks who had royal patronage and engaged in the construction of temples, harassing the peasants, and interfering with farming.[62]

The king also found ready allies among the palace attendants, who

---

60. *KS,* 11:20b–21a; *KSC,* 11:32b–33a.
61. *KSC,* 11:44a.
62. *KS,* 18:18a, 18:11a; *KSC,* 11:30b. People of the period openly acknowledged that "power rested with the eunuchs." *KSC,* 11:28b.

were in an obvious position, much like the eunuchs, to support the king. They worked with the king daily and attended to his needs. Many aristocratic youths had their first introductions to court politics and their initial training in government as palace attendants. However, during Ŭijong's reign the histories indicate many palace attendants were in fact eunuchs.[63] The censorate, perhaps bothered by these changes or fearful of their collusion with the king, on a number of occasions admonished these royal attendants and demanded the dismissal of some.[64] The histories also indicate that some palace attendants had even obtained their prominence through bribery.[65]

According to the sources, the palace attendants, rather than acting as a restraint on less-enlightened royal activities, abetted the king in his neglect of state affairs. Accompanying Ŭijong on his many journeys, the palace attendants are depicted as promoting an atmosphere of debauchery and intoxication. They also incurred fiscal irresponsibility by competing in offering precious gifts to the monarch. One entry in the histories, attempting to demonstrate the decadence of this group, relates:

All palace attendants compete in presenting precious gifts. The king gave the left division ten *kun* of white gold and sixty-five *kun* of red silk and the right division ten *kun* of white gold and ninety-five *kun* of red silk. At that time many influential men in the right division, by obtaining the eunuch's royal permission, sought many precious objects from public and private places. At the same time, they presented two choice horses. The left division, ashamed at being unable to equal them, borrowed five fine horses and presented them to the king. Later, unable to repay the debt, they were daily pressed for payment. Contemporaries laughed at them.[66]

Although the veracity of these facts cannot be denied, it is also clear that the palace attendants, like the eunuchs, were Ŭijong's agents and instrumental in carrying out his will.

The court, moreover, also won to its side many of the leading officials of the day. If Ŭijong's power had rested solely on assistance from eunuchs and palace attendants, his base of support would have been too confined to be effective. Throughout his rule Ŭijong always had several leading officials, often councilors of state, as his close confidants. Early in his reign he had the trusted cooperation of the eminent scholar Chŏng Sŭpmyŏng.[67] Kim Chonjung, introduced earlier as an opponent of the Chŏngan Im clan, was another close adviser to the king during the early part of Ŭijong's reign. Kim passed the state examination and reached the

63. See Yi Uch'ŏl, "Koryŏ sidae ŭi hwan'gwan e taehayo," *Sahak yŏn'gu*, no. 1 (1958):35.
64. *KS*, 17:38b; *KSC*, 11:14b, 11:30b.
65. *KSC*, 11:44a.
66. *KS*, 18:26a–b; *KSC*, 11:38b.
67. Chŏng Sŭpmyŏng died in 1151; see note 23, herein.

position of transmitter *(sǔngsǒn).*[68] Other men, such as Ch'oe Yunǔi, Kim Tonjung, and Hǒ Hungjae, affiliated themselves with Ǔijong and his rule.[69] Despite the impression provided by the dynastic histories, Ǔijong ruled through a much wider base of support than just eunuchs and palace attendants. To focus only on this narrow sector does an injustice to Ǔijong and perpetuates misconceptions about this reign.

Many members of the aristocracy willingly supported Ǔijong. He was the king. As the leader of the country, he not only carried considerable symbolic power and embodied legitimacy, but had great potential in executing affairs. Many leading aristocrats found their lives easier, and perhaps economically richer, by supporting the status quo and the king as well, and these people readily fell into the ranks behind the king. Other aristocrats also supported Ǔijong because they disliked the people opposing him and would prefer to ally with the royal party rather than the opposition.

The aristocracy, however, remained divided, and Ǔijong also had many adversaries. The resistance of the royal maternal family has already been mentioned. This group included not only the Chǒngan Im clan but also members of the Tongju Ch'oe clan, the Tongnae Sǒ clan, and later the Namp'yǒng Mun clan. Rivalry became particularly intense in 1151 and then in 1157 when Ǔijong exiled members of these clans. Opposition to the king also continued throughout the reign as the censorate voiced vigorous disapproval of numerous royal activities. Some aristocrats looked at the people allied to the king, such as eunuchs, and concluded the monarch was guilty by association. Others sided against the king because they opposed his rule in general and wanted changes in the power structure. Divisions in the aristocratic power structure were once again causing fissures in the Koryǒ ruling class. And as the differences increased, military personnel found opportunities to assume the role of arbiter.

### Status of Military Personnel

The role of the military as arbiters was not unique to Ǔijong's reign. The coup d'état of 1170 was in part the fruition of events of earlier periods. At the start of the eleventh century the Koryǒ dynasty confronted

68. *KS,* 123:3b–4b; *KSC,* 11:17b–18a.
69. Ch'oe yunǔi, a member of the prestigious Haeju Ch'oe clan, passed the state examination and became a tutor to Ǔijong's son, the crown prince. *Chōsen kinseki sōran,* vol. 1 (Seoul, 1933), pp. 388–390; *KS,* 99:25a–b; *KSC,* 11:32a–b. Kim Tonjung, the son of Kyǒngu Kim clansman Kim Pusik, as holder of the office of transmitter *(sǔngsǒn),* was close to Ǔijong. *KS,* 98:19b–21b. And so was Hǒ Hungjae, who earlier passed the state examination and under Ǔijong became executive *(p'yǒngjangsa). P'ahanjip* in *Koryǒ myǒng-hyǒnjip* (Seoul, 1971), 1:3b. See also, *KS,* 11:3b–4a; *KSC,* 11:47a.

several major invasions launched by the northern Khitan tribes, and without the preparations and defense offered by the military forces, the dynasty could have been overpowered. One result of these invasions was an increase in military awareness, and when some civil officials tried to limit military salaries in 1014, the military officers revolted. Although this coup lasted less than half a year, it was a manifestation both of general military discontent over the policy of civil supremacy and also of their revived political consciousness.

During the early Koryŏ period, there were several other major challenges to the authority of the throne that left the military with still greater involvement in the political arena. At the close of the eleventh century when several civil aristocrats vied for power, many military leaders found themselves settling the disturbance. In Injong's reign (1122–1146) military officers again were instrumental in effecting basic changes in the power structure. In 1124 military personnel attempted to assassinate Yi Chagyŏm, the de facto ruler of the kingdom. Although initially they failed, ultimately military assistance was crucial in defeating and removing Yi Chagyŏm from power by 1126.[70] Then, less than ten years later, with the Myoch'ŏng rebellion in 1135, military leadership again aided in crushing this major challenge and restoring peace to the country. As a result of these conflicts, the military became quite aware of the civil aristocracy's inability to settle pressing power disputes amicably, and the military leaders also gained a new consciousness of their own intrinsic power and potential to affect decisions. Yet they also discovered that although their potential was vast, they were constrained by the realities of the strict Koryŏ order.

During this period the political and economic status of the military officer was in flux. As mentioned earlier, some historians have argued that the military class experienced a slow rise in economic, social, and political prominence. This general advance in status brought a corresponding increase in aspirations, causing the military to revolt to enhance still further its position in the kingdom.[71] If one examines this argument, its validity becomes questionable. From the tenth century the dynasty distributed land allotments in favor of the civil officials and to the detriment of military officers.[72] In 1076 this discrepancy was corrected, advancing the highest military officer, the supreme general *(sang-changgun)*, to a level equal to his civilian counterpart in rank and in some

70. Kang, "The Development of the Korean Ruling Class," pp. 211, 270-278.
71. See note 10, herein.
72. The *chŏnsikwa,* literally, field and wood classification system, distributed land rent yields to all civil and military officials and other people who served the dynasty according to their positions in the government.

cases setting the land allotments in the military officer's favor. At the end of the tenth century the supreme general was in land grade five, and in Munjong's reign (1064–1083), some sixty years later, he had moved up to grade three. In real terms this meant that the supreme general received 130 *kyŏl* of land (80 *kyŏl* of paddy land and 50 *kyŏl* of woodland) under the old system, which was changed to 125 *kyŏl* of land (85 *kyŏl* of paddy land and 40 *kyŏl* of woodland) under the new. Although the military officer advanced on the scales, his actual land holdings did not increase.[73] A similar case can be made for the grand general *(tae-changgun)* and general *(changgun)*.

Adjustments were also made in stipend scales. In addition to land allotments, officials received specified amounts of rice every year. The dynasty also initially weighted these stipends to favor the civil official, but on changing the land allotment system the state adjusted these rice stipends to provide equal payments for officials of the same rank, be they military or civilian. The supreme general, a third *p'um* senior rank, received the same amount of salary as a minister *(sangsŏ)* in the six ministries who had the same *p'um* rank. Table 1 compares the salary scales of military officers and similarly ranked civilian officials in 1076.[74] The economic status of the military official relative to that of the civil official had improved since the start of the Koryŏ dynasty. However, the fundamental concept of civil supremacy still remained. The civilian ranks monopolized the top levels of all payment scales. One might also question the equality of land distributions. Although the military officers were receiving increased amounts of paddy land, what type of land were they actually receiving? Was it of the same quality as the land given to the civil officers? Probably not, although, with the available sources, no satisfactory answer can be found in these questions.[75]

If the military officer's economic status did not improve significantly, was he still able to obtain some gains in political or social status? Military officers, even though limited in number, did hold civil positions working in the ministries and parts of the Department of Ministries. Ranking military officers also could take advantage of the *ŭm* privilege and recommend men for military office. In these ways some men were

73. For an analysis of the changes in the *chŏnsikwa,* see Kang, "The Development of the Korean Ruling Class," p. 218, and Pyŏn, "Koryŏ muban yŏn'gu," pp. 375–376. One *kyŏl* of land equalled approximately ninety-six ares (0.96 hectares). See Kang Chinch'ŏl, "Traditional Land Tenure Relations in Korean Society: Ownership and Management," *Traditional Culture and Society of Korea,* p. 94, note 19. Ares incorrectly appears as acres.

74. See also, *KS,* 80:2a–6a, and Kang, "The Development of the Korean Ruling Class," p. 223.

75. Yi Kibaek does suggest that the military officers received land of inferior quality. See Yi Kibaek, "Korea—The Military Tradition," p. 21.

Table 1. Salaries of Koryŏ Military and Civilian Officials in 1076

| Rice Received | *P'um* Rank | Military Post | Civilian Post |
|---|---|---|---|
| 300.00 tu* | 3a‡ | sang-changgun | yukbu sangsŏ |
| 233.05 tu | 3b | tae-changgun | sangsŏ |
| 200.00 tu | 4a | changgun | sirang |
| 120.00 tu | 5a | chung nangjang | nangjung |
| 86.10 tu | 6a | nangjang | wŏnoerang |

* one *tu* equals 316 cubic inches.
‡ a = senior; b = junior.
Source: Adapted from Pyŏn T'aesŏp, "Koryŏ muban yŏn'gu," *Koryŏ chŏngch'i chedosa yŏn'gu* (Seoul, 1971), p. 378.

able to exercise political power. And as a result of events in the reigns of Injong and Ŭijong, there was a heightened consciousness among military officials of their potential in politics.

Still, even with these developments, when Koryŏ confronted serious internal and foreign attacks, the idea of civil supremacy was very much evident as the military officers were effectively barred from exercising their full power. In Ŭijong's reign, for example, the dynasty did not admit one military officer to the top decision-making body, the *chaesang*. Although the power and influence of the military leadership had increased, the state still denied officers access to the important political bodies of the kingdom.

Socially the status of the military officer was equally ambiguous. One cannot deny that biographies of men of military descent do start appearing in the *Koryŏsa* during the 1040s, a fact that might indicate some rise in their status.[76] Equally significant is the number of men from military families allowed into the civilian structure and advanced to top positions through civilian offices. Namp'yŏng Mun clansmen, Kigye No clansmen, and Ch'ungju Yang clansmen are just a few examples.[77] However, these families represented the elite of the military officer corps and presumably there was not so much of a social gap between them and the leading civilian families. Other examples can also be cited. In 1110 the dynasty instituted a military examination that established certain levels of competence for each rank. Through this examination, which enabled soldiers to be appointed on the basis of their skills, the professional standard and the social prestige of the military service increased. Twenty-three years later, however, civilian officials, jealous over the advances of

76. Pyŏn, "Koryŏ muban yŏn'gu," p. 347.
77. Ibid. and biographies of Mun Kŭkkyŏm in *KS*, 99:15b–19b; No Yongsun in *KS*, 100:6b–7a, and *Chōsen kinseki sōran*, vol. 1, p. 415; and Yang Wŏnjun in Yi Nanyŏng, *Han'guk kŭmsŏngmun ch'ubo*, pp. 145–146.

the military officials, forced the abandonment of these examinations.[78]
The functions the common soldiers performed also changed. No longer
handling only military matters, soldiers increasingly worked on labor
tasks such as digging ditches and on other public works projects. This
too represented a decline in the social status of the military class.[79] Not
only was the military officer's social recognition not rising, the common
soldier was in worse straits. For all these reasons the military undoubtedly chafed under civilian dominance.

The problems and conditions of Ŭijong's reign further exasperated
the military leadership and helped foment the coup of 1170. The differences between the two services were accentuated in this period as many
ranking civil officials accompanied Ŭijong on his countless trips. With
the king they would drink and relax, often refusing to allow their military
attendants relief from their guard duties. There was an expression of arrogance rarely seen in dynastic politics as the civil officials ridiculed and
belittled even high-ranking but hapless military officers. On one occasion
General Chŏng Chungbu, a stately man of some six feet and later a leader of the 1170 revolt, had his long grey beard burned as a practical joke
by a civil official from an elite aristocratic family.[80] Similar attacks on
military officers were not uncommon.

The eunuchs, with their new power, and their accomplices, the
palace attendants, instigated many disputes. The rise of eunuchs, who
often came from humble or socially less-prestigious families, was particularly abhorrent to the military clans. Although military officers were
subservient to civilian officials, they were nevertheless proud of their
family status and heritage. The military establishment became increasingly aggravated as the eunuchs centered jokes or character assassina-
tions on unsuspecting military officers. In 1156 a junior colonel (nang-
jang), Ch'oe Sukch'ŏng, angered at the churlish behavior of eunuch
Chŏng Ham and a civilian, Yi Wŏnŭng, announced his intention to kill
them both. His plot was discovered, however, and Sukch'ŏng was banished.[81] U Hagyu, another military official, in recollecting his father's
words, revealed a brewing discontent among the military when he said,
"My father once warned, 'The military officials have seen injustices for
too long. Is it possible for them not to be indignant?' "[82]

    78. Pyŏn, "Koryŏ muban yŏn'gu," pp. 366–367.
    79. Yi Kibaek, "Koryŏ kunbanje haŭi kunin" in Koryŏ pyŏngjesa yŏn'gu, p. 289 and
note 9.
    80. KS, 128:1b.
    81. Ibid., 122:12a; KSC, 11:19b.
    82. KS, 100:6a–b; KSC, 12:41b.

### The 1170 Coup d'État

As early as 1164 the military officials started to consider drastic measures to rectify their grievances. In the spring of that year the king, on an excursion to the countryside, was appreciating the scenery with civilian scholars by singing and drinking. The military escorts, generals and soldiers alike, were fatigued by constant jaunts like this and burned with indignation. It was at this time that Chŏng Chungbu, the commanding general of the royal guards, and other military officers first considered a military coup d'état.[83] Although they made no definite plans at the time, as the years progressed they became increasingly desperate and determined to act.

To the military leaders it appeared that the king, his close officials, and attendants paid less and less attention to state affairs and more attention to their personal enjoyment and relaxation, with the military officials often grossly neglected. Moreover, the military officers frequently had to take blame and punishment for the actions of their civilian counterparts. On one royal excursion, a civilian official's horse lost its footing, causing a stray arrow to fall near the royal coach. Rather than accept responsibility for the mishap, the man remained silent and allowed the king to believe that the military officers had made an attempt on his life. The guiltless officers in question were banished.[84] After another such party, two military officers, Yi Ŭibang and Yi Ko, voiced the indignation that their fellow officers had suppressed too long: "Now the civilian officials are haughty, drunk, and full, but the military men are hungry and troubled. How long can this be tolerated?" Chŏng Chungbu, still resenting the fact that his beard had been burned, seized the opportunity to complete plans for a revolt.[85]

Chŏng, the leader of the 1170 coup d'état, was a member of the Haeju Chŏng clan, which had already produced, several decades earlier, a famous general—Chŏng Chŏngsuk—who not only helped suppress the Myoch'ŏng revolt, but advanced to the second *p'um* rank and took the semihonorary civilian title of *chwabogya*.[86] Chungbu, holding a leading post in the military structure, must have been quite aware of the potential strength of the military. He undoubtedly recalled that in the past military men like his relative Chŏngsuk had been called to render service when the aristocratic civilian leaders were unable to correct crises brewing in the

83. *KS,* 128:2a; *KSC,* 11:35a–b.
84. *KSC,* 11:40a–41a.
85. *KS,* 128:2a; *KSC,* 11:49a.
86. Yi Nanyŏng, *Han'guk kŭmsŏngmun ch'ubo,* p. 118; *KS,* 98:3b.

dynasty. Moreover the military was once brave enough to initiate action on its own to redress grievances when arrogant civilian authorities had mistreated and abused them. Military officers had also played very prominent roles in checking foreign invaders and bringing settlements when feuding civil officials resorted to armed confrontation. Chŏng, besides being aware of the traditions of the military, was also quite familiar with the unsettled conditions prevailing at the court. His son's father-in-law, Kim Iyŏng, for example, had been banished. Chŏng watched the censorate's powc erode as eunuchs and palace attendants interfered with the management of state affairs. He also saw the growing arrogance of the officials who flocked to the king.

The schism within the civil structure became increasingly visible. Ŭijong surrounded himself with willing supporters, whether they be councilors of state, eunuchs, or palace attendants. Others, perhaps spurned by these people or disillusioned with state affairs, began to turn away, and some looked to the military as a possible last resort to bring an end to the rapidly degenerating state of affairs. The tenuous ties between the Prince Kyŏng-Chŏngan Im clan and the military have already been suggested. Certainly if there had not been divisions among the civilian officials, and if there had not been a core of ranking officials equally disenchanted with court activities, chances for the success of a military coup d'état would have been greatly diminished, if not nil. By the summer of 1170, these were the prime forces moving the kingdom toward an unavoidable conflict. Then in the eighth month, on a signal from General Chŏng Chungbu, the military struck, killing or banishing more than fifty officials, eunuchs, and palace attendants and forcing Ŭijong to abdicate.[87]

### Aftermath of the Coup

To comprehend the ramifications of this incident, a careful investigation of both the men who were removed from office and the men who advanced with the coup d'état is essential. Through this analysis, the role of both military and civilian officials will become apparent. To assure the success of their revolt, the military elicited the cooperation and aid of civilian officials. It was the civilian officials who had been critical of Ŭijong and his associates who generally advanced to prominence after the coup and worked with the military establishment. However, they played supplementary roles.

Military officers commanded the revolt with Yi Ko, Yi Ŭibang, and Chŏng Chungbu, all members of the royal guard, as the prime instiga-

87. *KS*, 128:2a–3a; *KSC*, 11:51a–52a.

tors. Chŏng, as general, carried esteem; the other conspirators were not as distinguished. At least forty-seven men were targets of the purge initiated at this time (see Table 2). Many of those ousted were eunuchs, palace attendants, and civil officials who had clustered around Ŭijong and participated in the royal adventures. The military leaders removed at least twelve palace attendants from the power structure and dismissed an additional ten nameless palace attendants.[88] The palace attendants were by far the largest single group to be ousted. During Ŭijong's reign, the palace attendants continually interfered in court affairs. Always in attendance on the king, they were clearly associated with Ŭijong as his closest advisers and by this had incurred the enmity not just of the military leadership but of many civilians as well. In addition to the palace attendants, thirteen other men who had achieved their positions through devious means, or who had contributed to misgovernment during Ŭijong's reign, were also removed. Many of these people were eunuchs and others were high-ranking officials, and like the palace attendants, they were purged. This entire group had harassed the soldiers and officers for many years. They caused Chŏng Chungbu and his followers, as well as many civilian officials, to burn with indignation and shame. Now they were the target of reprisals.

The next largest group removed were officials associated with military policy. Six members of the Security Council (Ch'umirwŏn) and three members of the Ministry of Military Affairs (Pyŏngbu) were victims of the 1170 revolt. In addition, four former military commissioners *(pyŏngmasa)* were also discharged. It has been suggested that the civilian officials who held this last post had considerable military power.[89] Thus it was essential to remove them and other civil officials in military agencies not only to secure absolute control over the dynastic military structure but to be free from possible civilian countercoups. It is noteworthy that the modest goals of the first major military revolt in 1014 had been obstructed by just such a countercoup.

Only three councilors of state out of a possible eleven were removed, and they were close associates of Ŭijong.[90] Nine members of the lower ranks of the Security Council and Royal Secretariat and Chancellery (Chungsŏmunhasŏng) were also dismissed. The Security Council discussed matters of national defense, and officials in the lower ranks of the Royal Secretariat and Chancellery were important in daily remonstrance

88. *KSC,* 11:55a.
89. Suematsu Yasukazu, "Kōrai heibashi ko," *Tōyō gakuhō,* 39, no. 1 (1956), and *Seikyū sisō* (Tokyo, 1968), p. 207.
90. They were Ch'oe Yuch'ing, Ch'oe On, and Hŏ Hungjae. See Shultz, "Institutional Developments in Korea under the Ch'oe House," pp. 31–35.

Table 2. Men Removed from Power in the Coup d'État of 1170

| Name | Origin | Office Held | Miscellaneous |
|------|--------|-------------|---------------|
| Chin Hyŏn'gwang | | naesi sogyŏng | |
| Chin Yunsŭng | | pyŏngbusirang | |
| Ch'oe Ch'i | | wŏnoerang | |
| Ch'oe Ch'un | | sogyŏng | |
| Ch'oe Hyŏn | | naesi sogyŏng | |
| Ch'oe On | Chiksan | chich'umirwŏnsa | father: Hangjae; partied with king; formerly a pyŏngmasa |
| Ch'oe Tongsik | | kamch'alŏsa | |
| Ch'oe Yuch'ing | | p'yŏngjangsa | partied with king |
| Ch'oe Yunsŏ | Haeju | taebusogyŏng | |
| Cho Mun'gwi | | wiwisogyŏng | |
| Cho Munjin | | sirang | passed examination |
| Cho Tonghŭi | | pyŏngbusirang | |
| Chŏn Ch'iyu | | pongŏ | |
| Han Nŏe | | kigŏju | |
| Hŏ Chadan | | taesasŏng | |
| Hŏ Hongjae | | p'anibusa | passed examination; formerly a pyŏngmasa, chigonggŏ |
| Im Chongsik | | ubusŭngsŏn | partied with king |
| Kang Ch'ŏgyung | | tosŏng nangjung | |
| Kang Ch'ŏyak | | pyŏngbu nangjung | |
| Kim Chagi | | sach'ŏn'gam | a diviner |
| Kim Kisin · | | ŏsajapdan | |
| Kim Kŏsil | | haenggung pyŏlgam | naesi |
| Kim Kwang | | naesi chihu | |
| Kim Kwangjung | Kwangyang | pisŏgam | passed examination; formerly a pyŏngmasa, chigonggŏ |
| Kim Sujang | | pyŏlgam | |
| Kim Tonjung | Kyŏngju | sŭngsŏn | passed examination; father: Pusik |
| Kim Tonsi | Kyŏngju | săngsŏ | passed examination; father: Pusik |
| Pae Chin | | chihu | father: Kyŏngsŏng |
| Pae Yŏn | | naesi chihu | father: Kyŏngsŏng |
| Paek Chadan | | | eunuch |
| Pak Pogyun | | taebusogyŏng | |
| Pak Yun'gong | | siŏsa | naesi |
| Sŏ Sun | | tongchich'umirwŏnsa | formerly a pyŏngmasa, chigonggŏ |
| Ŭm Chungin | | sach'ŏn'gam | |
| Wang Kwangch'wi | | | eunuch |
| Yang Sunjŏng | | ch'umirwŏnsa | |
| Yi Chisim | | kukchagam taesasŏng | passed examination; chigonggŏ |

Table 2. *(continued)*

| Name | Origin | Office Held | Miscellaneous |
|------|--------|-------------|---------------|
| Yi Inbo | | wŏnoerang | |
| Yi Pokki | | chiŏsadaesa | partied with king |
| Yi Set'ong | | sŭngsŏn | |
| Yi Tangju | | naesi | |
| Yi Yunsu | | | son: Yi Kyubo |
| Yŏng Ŭi | | naesisaryong | father earlier banished; mother descended from traitor |
| Yu Ikkyŏm | | chihu | |
| Yun Chongak | P'ap'yŏng | taebujubu | passed examination; father: Inch'ŏm |
| Yun Sunsin | P'ap'yŏng | ibusirang | passed examination; father: Ŏni; also known as Tosin |
| Yu Pangŭi | | naesi | |
| Total Removed: 47 | | | |
|   naesi | 12 | | |
|   members of Ch'umirwŏn | 6 | | |
|   members of Pyŏngbu | 3 | | |
|   members of Ŏsadae | 4 | | |
|   pyŏngmasa | 4 | | |
|   men who passed examination | 8 | | |
|   others | 10 | | |

and drafting criticism of policy. The Censorate (Ŏsadae), which was co-opted by Ŭijong during the last seven years of his rule, was also affected with four of its nine ranking members demoted or killed. The Institute of Astronomical Observation (Sach'ŏndae), which was in charge of reporting celestial changes and remonstrance through the observation of natural events, similarly had two of its members dismissed.

It is apparent that the military leadership did not ruthlessly slaughter all civilians in the 1170 revolt, as often charged, but rather the leaders were generally quite selective in whom they chose to purge. The list of victims from the P'ap'yŏng Yun clan underscores this point. Yun Inch'ŏm survived the coup and during Myŏngjong's reign (1170–1197) advanced to a position of prestige, but Inch'ŏm's brother, Tosin, and his son, Chongak, both were killed in the revolt. Lax officials who were guilty of mismanagement or extreme ostentation during Ŭijong's rule were the victims of the revolt, while those officials who were dedicated servants and honest in their administration often survived. Coupled with this element that bespeaks reform was the military leadership's desire, once in power, to exercise full control over the military establishment as well as the formulation of military power.

Not one military officer was dismissed during the initial stages of the revolt. Although reform of the civil structure was an important motive of the coup, it did not spread to affect the military elements. This indicates that although civilian support was crucial, there were still tensions present between military and some civilian personnel, and this was one cause of the revolt.

Through an investigation of the men who advanced in the early years after the revolt, the character of the revolt becomes still clearer. Even though the Chungbang, a body of generals, became the major center for dynastic decision-making, once the military leadership was firmly established in Myŏngjong's reign, the civil structure was still instrumental in effecting policy. As the Koryŏ civil bureaucracy was used to administer the country, it was the civil structure that brought a sense of continuity as well as a sense of legitimacy to military rule. An examination of identifiable personnel in the dynastic civil structure thus will illustrate novel aspects of the 1170 revolt.

Forty-three men are identified among those who might have dominated the government in the first five years of Myŏngjong's reign (see Table 3). Only eight (19 percent) were recorded as having military ranks, while thirty-four (79 percent) were active in the civilian branch. One man's service is unknown. Of the civilian officials found, twenty-one (62 percent) were identified positively as having passed the civil service examination. This percentage is clearly half of the entire group. The lineages of many of these men are unknown, but at least nineteen (44 percent) had fathers who held the fifth rank or higher in the dynastic structure prior to 1170. Probably this figure would be still higher if there were complete records. Twelve of the men, or 28 percent, were found also to have had grandfathers in the fifth rank or higher. A number of individuals, such as Ch'oe Yuch'ŏng, whose immediate ancestry lay in powerful regional families, also continued to hold positions. This suggests that strong provincial elite clans, first seen in Injong's reign and then seen again as a possible focal point of loyalty for one group during Ŭijong's rule, still carried political potential in Myŏngjong's reign. On the other hand, not a single person of humble origins appeared in the dynastic ranks. In assessing these figures, it becomes apparent that in spite of the potential for men of ordinary, commoner origins to enter the dynastic bureaucracy, if one's father had already had some dynastic service, chances of success remained strong. If one had successfully completed the state examination, he was given more assurance of a ranking appointment.

These trends are underscored by the composition of the elite Council of State. Among the thirteen councilors of state listed at this time, four

Table 3. Composition of Civil Structure During the First Five Years of Myŏngjong's Reign (1170–1175)

| Name | Service | Examination | Background | Miscellaneous |
|---|---|---|---|---|
| Chaesang | | | | |
| Chungsŏmunhasŏng | | | | |
| Kyŏng Chin | M | | | 2 |
| Yang Suk | M | | | 1, 2 |
| Chŏng Chungbu | M | | A | 1, 3 |
| Chin Chun | M | | AA | 3 |
| No Yŏngsun | C | | A | |
| Sŏ Kong | C | | AA | |
| Yun Inch'ŏm | C | E | AA | 3 |
| Yi Kongsŭng | C | E | A | |
| Yi Kwangjin | C | | AA | |
| Ch'umirwŏn | | | | |
| Im Kŭkch'ung | C | E | A | |
| Ch'oe Yuch'ŏng | C | E | A | |
| Han Ch'wi | C | E | | |
| Kyŏng Chin | M | | | 1 |
| Chin Chun | M | | AA | 2 |
| Yun Inch'ŏm | C | E | AA | |
| Kim Ch'ŏn | C | E | A | 2 |
| Chungsŏmunhasŏng (3–7 *p'um* grade) | | | | |
| Yi Soung | C | | | |
| Kwak Yangsŏn | C | E | | |
| Kim Podang | C | | AA | |
| Ch'oe Yŏhae | C | E | | |
| Wang Segyŏng | C | E | A | |
| Im Minbi | C | E | A | |
| Ch'oe Tang | C | E | AA | |
| Ch'oe Uch'ŏng | C | E | | |
| Han Ŏn'guk | C | E | | |
| Kim Hwayun | C | E | | |
| Ch'umirwŏn (3–7 *p'um* grade) | | | | |
| Ki T'aksŏng | M | | | 2 |
| Song Yuin | M | | | |
| Yi Kwangjŏng | M | | | |
| Yi Ŭibang | M | | | |
| Yi Chunŭi | M | | | |
| Mun Kŭkkyŏm | C | E | AA | |
| Min Yŏngmo | C | E | AA | 2 |
| Kim Ch'ŏn | C | E | AA | |
| Sangsŏdosŏng | | | | |
| Yi Munjŏ | C | | AA | 2 |
| Yi Chimyŏng | C | E | | |
| Kim Sŏngmi | ? | | | |
| Six Ministries | | | | |
| Personnel | | | | |
| Yi Munjŏ | C | | AA | 1 |
| Ch'oe Yuch'ŏng | C | E | A | |
| Public Works | | | | |
| Kim Podang | C | | AA | |
| Yu Ŭnggyu | C | | A | |

## Table 3. *(continued)*

| Name | Service | Examination | Background | Miscellaneous |
|---|---|---|---|---|
| **Punishments** | | | | |
| Min Yŏngmo | C | E | AA | 1 |
| **Military** | | | | |
| Yi Ŭibang | M | | | |
| Cho Wich'ong | C | | | |
| Ham Yuil | C | | | |
| **Rites** | | | | |
| Yi Ŭngch'o | C | E | AA | |
| Chang Ingmyŏng | C | | | |
| Ch'oe Kyun | C | E | | |
| Ch'oe Yuch'ŏng | C | E | A | 3 |
| Mun Kŭkkyŏm | C | E | AA | |
| **Unclear** | | | | |
| Song Sungbu | C | | | |
| Chang Ch'ungŭi | C | E | A | |
| **Ŏsadae** | | | | |
| Ki T'aksŏng | M | | | 1 |
| Yi Kwangjŏng | M | | | |
| Yi Ŭngjang | C | | AA | |
| Ch'oe Ch'ŏkkyŏng | C | E | | |
| Chin Kwangin | C | E | | |
| **Chingonggŏ** | | | | |
| Kwak Yangsŏn | C | E | | |
| Kim Hwayun | C | E | | |
| Yun Inch'ŏm | C | E | AA | |
| Han Ŏn'guk | C | E | | |
| Han Ch'wi | C | E | | |
| Kim Ch'ŏn | C | E | AA | |
| Mun Kŭkkyŏm | C | E | AA | |
| Min Yŏngmo | C | E | AA | |

| | |
|---|---|
| Total number of officials | 43 |
| Civil Officials | 34 (79%) |
| Military Officials | 8 (19%) |
| Unknown | 1 ( 2%) |
| Civil officials who had passed the examination | 21 (62%) |
| All other civil officials | 13 (38%) |
| Officials whose father was fifth *p'um* or higher | 19 (44%) |
| Of the above, those whose grandfathers were also fifth *p'um* or higher | 12 (28%) |
| All other officials | 24 (56%) |

Note: The basic and summary sections of Table 3 are not comparable because officials may be listed more than once in the former.

KEY: C - civilian
  M - military
  ? - unknown
  E - passed examination
  A - father fifth *p'um* or higher
  AA - father and grandfather fifth *p'um* or higher
  Numbers under miscellaneous indicate progression in advancement.

were products of the military service and the remaining nine were civilians. Although military officers had not previously served as councilors of state, these men were all from well-known families, with three of the four coming from clans that had produced distinguished generals during earlier reigns. Yang Suk, for example, had even held a civil position during Ŭijong's reign. Of the nine civilians, at least five had passed the state examination, and eight were from families with previous dynastic service. Such men as Im Kŭkch'ung, Ch'oe Yuch'ŏng, and Yun Inch'ŏm were promoted to councilor of state soon after the coup. The Kyŏngju Kim, Kyŏngwŏn Yi, and Ich'ŏn Sŏ clans were also represented. Clearly the elite character of the councilors of state had not been radically changed by the coup.

The military leaders do not seem to have tried to dominate any one area in the bureaucracy either. As with the councilors of state, the important lower posts of the Security Council were almost equally divided between civilian and military families. In the Ministry of Military Affairs there was only one military officer, Yi Ŭibang. But Yi was one of the ringleaders of the coup and undoubtedly through this position was able to dictate the work of the ministry, including promotions for many.

For a variety of reasons, civilians participated in the new regime. Even though the new leaders forced Ŭijong to abdicate and replaced him with Myŏngjong, the court was still influential in choosing some men. Several of Myŏngjong's friends, such as Min Yŏngmo and Ch'oe Yŏhae, as well as royal relatives, received their positions in part because of their ties with the king.[91] And, as mentioned earlier, civilians still lent a sense of legitimacy and ran the administration.

The "anti-royal clique" that Ŭijong had purged in 1157 returned to power following the coup. Shortly after the revolt, the histories relate, the leadership summoned Kim Iyŏng, Yu Chaksŭng, and Chŏng Sŏ to the capital and gave them office land.[92] At about the same time, Ch'oe Yuch'ŏng and Im Kŭkch'ung (Kŭkchŏng's brother) became councilors of state. These things alone might appear insignificant, but when considered together with the rise to prominence of this whole group and recalling that this clique did have ties with the military, it appears that these men worked to enhance the military's success. Certainly without their support, the coup might have been far less successful.[93]

The revolt was to an important degree a product of the political tensions that had intensified in Ŭijong's reign. The decline in the status of the military is only one aspect. Ŭijong's search for independence

91. *KS,* 101:1a–2a, 101:7a–8a; *KSC,* 13:32a–b, 13:11b–12a.
92. *KS,* 19:12b, 90:39a; *KSC,* 11:58a.
93. Prince Kyŏng, Ŭijong's early antagonist, was passed over in succession and instead his younger brother Ho was made king and ascended the throne as Myŏngjong.

ironically destroyed him. He tormented powerful antagonists, and the debauchery and arrogance of his court officials, eunuchs, and palace attendants inflamed the passions of many civilian and military officials. Cleavages within the court, which set the king against his brothers and his own mother, further marred the politics of the age. The dynastic political institutions were not able to provide a check either, as the remonstrances of the censorial bodies, perhaps inspired by political intrigue and certainly overstressed, passed unheeded. Under mounting tension, the grievances of the military leaders and the disillusionment of the civilian scholars coalesced into the 1170 military coup d'état.

# The Shifting Strategic Value of Korea, 1942–1950

*Masao Okonogi*
KEIO UNIVERSITY

IF an analogy may be made between the situation in Europe after World War II and that after the Napoleonic Wars, as George Kennan and Ernest May have, then a similar analogy may be made between the situation in East Asia after the last world war and that after the Sino-Japanese War, for the collapse of the Japanese empire created a tremendous power vacuum running from Manchuria through Korea to Japan proper that was very similar to the vacuum created by the defeat of the Ch'ing dynasty in the Sino-Japanese War.[1] The cold war in postwar East Asia, in this sense, is similar in nature to that in Europe, on the one hand, while it is historically similar to the time period from the Sino-Japanese War to the Russo-Japanese War, on the other.

Ironically, after World War II the U.S., by overthrowing Japanese militarism, occupying Japan and south Korea, and committing itself to the independence of Korea, had no alternative but to succeed to the geopolitical position once occupied by Japan. This position was taken without any firm strategic plan. As Louis Halle has pointed out, U.S. succession to this position implied that the more the U.S. became involved with the security of this region, the more enmity would grow between the U.S. and Japan's traditional adversaries.[2] To borrow the words of George Kennan, who analyzed the confrontation between Japan and Russia in

---

1. See George F. Kennan, "The Passing of the Cold War," lecture, Tokyo, June 19, 1964, *Amerika Gaiko no kihon mondai* (Tokyo, 1965), p. 6; Ernest R. May *"Lessons" of the Past: The Use and Misuse of History in American Foreign Policy* (New York, 1973), p. 16. In accuracy, it should be noted that the condition brought forth in East Asia after the Sino-Japanese war stemmed from the opening of Korea, because its opening per se suggested the appearance of a power vacuum.

2. Louis J. Halle, *The Cold War as History* (London: 1970), pp. 191–192.

the early twentieth century: "It was an inevitable development, at that point in history," for the U.S. and the Soviet Union "to encounter and be confronted with each other in one form or another, and to settle their spheres of influence in Manchuria and Korea."[3]

Our concern here is with the asymmetric nature of the cold war in Europe and Asia. However, this is a very difficult question. First of all, this asymmetric feature is closely associated with the existence of domestic conflict in the areas concerned. As typically illustrated in Korea, China, and Indochina, after World War II in Asia there existed vertical domestic conflicts differing from the horizontal ones between the West and the East. Because of the interaction of these two types of conflict, the existence of domestic power struggles played a considerable role in both the internalization of international conflict and the internationalization of domestic confrontations. Second, the asymmetry is also related to a geographical factor. It is well known that the Soviet Union has traditionally perceived its own security in spacial terms while the United States has tended to view its security in institutional terms.[4] Nevertheless, this antagonism in security concepts did not develop into a hot war in the centers of Europe or the Asian continent because the geographic conditions were lacking. The exceptions were the two peninsulas thrusting out from the Asian continent, Korea and Indochina, where there remained room for both the U.S. and the Soviet Union to intervene directly or indirectly. In addition, these areas were the strategic points from which it was possible to exercise influence on the heart of the continent from its circumference, and to advance from the continent out to sea. In this context, it was Greece, despite the intense conflict over Berlin, that had the potential for transforming the cold war into a hot war in Europe. This consideration is quite suggestive.[5]

I have already presented a dissertation that deals with the first point.[6] Thus, this discussion will focus on the second point, how the U.S., the Soviet Union, and China evaluated the strategic value of the Korean peninsula, and how they attempted to deal with the power vacuum created there. Therefore, this article does not necessarily concentrate on any specific aspect of the Korean War. Instead, it is designed to reappraise the character of the war by taking a bird's-eye view of the strategic

3. George F. Kennan, "The Russo-Japanese War, an American View," lecture, Tokyo, June 17, 1964, *Amerika Gaiko*, p. 75.

4. John L. Gaddis, *Russia, the Soviet Union and the United States* (New York, 1978), p. 176.

5. See Norman B. Hannh, "The Asian Boundaries of Coexistence," in Lynn Miller and Ronald Pruessen, eds., *Reflections on the Cold War* (Philadelphia, Penn., 1974), p. 96.

6. See Masao Okonogi, "The Domestic Roots of the Korean War," in Yōnosuke Nagai and Akira Iriye, eds., *The Origins of the Cold War in Asia* (Tokyo, 1977), pp. 299–320.

value of the Korean peninsula, a duality that has an amphibious character.[7] Such an expression may not be scientific; the U.S. is not considered
to be a sea power, and the Soviet Union and China are not considered
land powers. However, this characterization is still permissible, for, as
Marshall Shulman has urged, "The Korean War is one of those events
which confirms the description of international relations as an art rather
than a science."[8]

### I. Trusteeship: Joint Administration by the Four Powers

It is well known that, as early as March, 1943, President Franklin D.
Roosevelt told British Foreign Secretary Anthony Eden about the international trusteeship that he envisioned for Korea.[9] After acquiring informal approval from Joseph Stalin at Teheran and Yalta, this plan remained pivotal in U.S. policy toward Korea until the summer of 1947.
However, little attention has been paid to the fact that Roosevelt's plan
was a product of Wilsonian idealism, as crystalized in the announcement
in Cairo that "in due course Korea shall become free and independent,"
at the same time that it reflected his deep concern for the geopolitical position of the Korean peninsula. To understand the geopolitical aspect, it
is essential to go back to the Roosevelt-Soong conference in the spring of
1942.

It was, as a matter of fact, the Chinese nationalists who were most
concerned about the future course of Korea during the Second World
War. China's move to promote an independent Korea had already begun
by the time the war in the Pacific broke out. This is illustrated by the fact
that on February 25, 1942, Tsiang Ting-fu, director of the Political Affairs Department of the Executive Yuan, applauded Roosevelt's February 24 radio address, which had referred to Korea, and officially expressed China's desire to recognize an independent Korea.[10] On March
22, Sun Fo, president of the Legislative Yuan, also took up the issue of
Korean independence in an address to the Association of Oriental Culture and others; he appealed for support for Korea's independence and
recognition of its provisional government.[11] Furthermore, China made

7. This point will be discussed independently in the Appendix, herein.
8. Marshall D. Shulman, *Stalin's Foreign Policy Reappraised* (Cambridge, Mass., 1963),
p. 139.
9. On the Korean problem during wartime conferences, see Soon Sung Cho, *Korea in
World Politics, 1940–1950: An Evaluation of American Responsibility* (Berkeley, Cal.,
1967), pp. 13–58.
10. *Ta-kung-pao,* February 25, 1942.
11. The Ambassador in China (Gauss) to the Secretary of State, March 28, 1942, U.S.
Department of State, *Foreign Relations of the United States, 1942: China* (Washington:
1956), pp. 730–731. (Hereafter cited as *FR.* Special subseries, such as the one on China, will
be identified; all other volumes will be identified by volume number and year only.)

efforts which were temporarily to bear fruit in the spring of 1942, to unify the two separate, bitterly opposed Korean independence movements in China.[12]

At a conference on April 8, Chinese Minister of Foreign Affairs, T. V. Soong, handed personally to Roosevelt a memorandum that made two proposals in support of Korean independence.[13] The first was to arm the 50,000-man Korean irregular army in north China and make the army the center of all Korean revolutionary activities. The second proposed that the Pacific War Council announce, at some opportune moment, its determination to effect the independence of Korea, and, either simultaneously or at some later time, recognize the Korean provisional government. This memo also warned that the Russian Far East Army in Siberia had for many years incorporated two or three regiments of Koreans.

Unquestionably, Soong's proposal to work for Korean independence and to recognize the Provisional Government of the Republic of Korea in Chungking was part of China's attempt to prevent the penetration of Russian influence into China's peripheral areas. In addition to the fact that Korea was in an area where disputes had traditionally arisen between Russia and China, events since the Sino-Japanese War had proved that Korea was an area of great significance for the security of Manchuria and north China. Therefore, it is no exaggeration to say that nothing would threaten China more than the prediction that the Soviet Union would establish a puppet government in Korea. Such concern on the Chinese side continued to be the main subject of Sino-Soviet relations during the following years.[14]

What, then, was Roosevelt's response to Soong's proposal? Responding to the president's request, Acting Secretary of State Sumner Welles, in his recommendation of April 13, supported assistance in organizing and equipping a Korean irregular army, but asserted that it was still premature for the Pacific War Council to announce its determination to effect the independence of Korea.[15] Welles gave two reasons for this: first, since the tide of the war was in Japan's favor, the council's statement would lack validity and it could not be expected to be effective;

12. See Ch'u Hŏn-su, "Chungil chŏnjaeng kwa imjŏng ŭi kunsa hwaldong" [Military activities of the Korean Provisional Government during the Sino-Japanese War, 1937–1945], *Asea hakbo* 9, pp. 26–27.

13. Memorandum by the Chinese Minister of Foreign Affairs (Soong), *FR, 1942,* vol. 1 (Washington: 1960), pp. 868–869.

14. Memorandum by Mr. O. Edmund Clubb of the Division of Chinese Affairs, May 19, 1944, *FR, 1944,* vol. 6 (Washington: 1967), pp. 785–793.

15. The Acting Secretary of State to President Roosevelt, April 13, 1942, *FR, 1942,* vol. 1, pp. 870–872.

and second, the failure of negotiations between the British and the people of India regarding India's independence was hampering the announcement of a broad policy of general liberation. According to Soong's report to his home government on April 16, Roosevelt followed a similar line of reasoning by stating that Korea's independence must be recognized at the proper time, and that the declaration of Korea's independence should coincide with the complete settlement of the India problem.[16]

Nevertheless, such a response by no means implied that the U.S. attached little importance to the enmity between China and the Soviet Union over the matter of Korean independence. On April 10, Ambassador to China Clarence Gauss reported to Secretary of State Cordell Hull that the gist of the issue in recognizing the provisional government was how the Soviet Union and Great Britain would react.[17] Also, Hull's memo to the president on April 29 pointed out: "There remains the possibility, in case the 'Korean Provisional Government' in Chungking is recognized by the Chinese Government, that the Soviet Union may support some other Korean group associated ideologically with the Soviet Union. The Chinese Government may be motivated . . . by a wish to nip in the bud the development of any Soviet-supported Korean group."[18] Hull ordered Gauss, when he relayed the foregoing comments to the Chinese government, to "emphasize that we are aware of the fact that geographical and racial factors render the question under reference of more immediate concern to China than to the United States . . . [and] that, if the Chinese should accord recognition to a Provisional Government of Korea, this Government would of course expect to re-examine its position in the light of that new step."[19]

Given such views, one can understand how subtle the American position was concerning this issue. In other words, Roosevelt proposed, on March 27, 1943, that "Korea might be placed under an international trusteeship, with China, the United States and one or two other countries participating," because of the diplomatic necessity of taking into account the interests of China, the Soviet Union, and Great Britain.[20] Therefore, this remark was the combined outcome of Roosevelt's ideal-

16. Chang Ch'ün and Huang Shao-ku, *Chiang tsung-t'ung wei tzu-yu chêng-i yü hê-píng êrh fên mên shu-lüeh* (Taipei: 1966), p. 280.
17. The Ambassador in China (Gauss) to the Secretary of State, April 10, 1942, *FR, 1942*, vol. 1, p. 869.
18. Memorandum by the Secretary of State to President Roosevelt, April 29, 1942, ibid., p. 873.
19. The Secretary of State to the Ambassador in China, May 1, 1942, ibid., pp. 873-875.
20. Memorandum of Conversation, by the Secretary of State, March 27, 1943, *FR, 1943*, vol. 3 (Washington: 1963), p. 37.

ism, reflected later in his call for "self-determination" in the Cairo declaration, and his concept of power politics, as reflected in his proposal
for joint administration by the Big Four. In this sense, one can agree with
Barton Bernstein's conclusion: "Never a dedicated internationalist committed to collective security, Roosevelt had not rejected the concept of
the 'Four Policemen' when he supported the United Nations."[21]

With respect to the U.S. role in the international administration of
Korea, only a few inferences can be drawn from such diverse sources as
the study prepared by the Inter-Divisional Area Committee on the Far
East at the request of the navy and the army after the Teheran Conference, the briefing-book paper readied for the president on the eve of the
Yalta Conference, and some documents prepared for the Potsdam Conference after Roosevelt's death. Yet, remarkably enough, all these documents showed a deep concern for the antagonism that existed between
Chinese and Soviet interests. For instance, the briefing-book paper for
the Yalta Conference stated that unilateral action by either party would
bring forth "serious political repercussions," while the study prepared
after the Teheran Conference asserted that "in any case there should be
no mandate for the United States alone."[22] This opposition to unilateral
action was a principal reason for the joint administration of Korea by the
Big Four as proposed in Roosevelt's plan. Moreover, this principle was
applicable not only in political actions but also in military operations.
This may be seen best in the following judgment by the military authorities at the time of the Potsdam Conference:

Various countries, especially China, the Soviet Union, Great Britain and the
United States, have an interest in Korea, either because of common frontiers
or because of Korea's strategic position, which vitally influences the peace
and security of the Far East. No one of these countries would wish to see any
one nation acquire a predominant position in Korea. . . . For these reasons it
is considered politically inadvisable for any one of the interested countries
alone to invade Korea for the purpose of driving out the Japanese. If it is
militarily feasible, therefore, it is believed advisable that the invading forces
be composed of units from the various interested countries, under a single
over-all Allied command.[23]

The remaining question is to what extent Roosevelt's plan reflected
American interests as they were related to the strategic value of the Kore-

21. Barton J. Bernstein, ed., *The Atomic Bomb, The Critical Issues,* (Boston, 1976),
p. 100.
22. Post-War Status of Korea, Briefing Book Paper, *FR: The Conferences at Malta and
Yalta, 1945* (Washington, 1955), p. 359; Memorandum prepared by the Inter-Divisional
Area Committee on the Far East, May 4, 1944; *FR, 1944,* vol. 5 (Washington, 1965), p.
1241.
23. Relationship of the Soviet Union to the war against Japan, No. 605, Briefing Book
Paper, *FR: The Conference of Berlin (The Potsdam Conference), 1945,* vol. 1 (Washington: 1960), pp. 925–926.

an peninsula. It is almost impossible to extract this answer, but one with shrewd insight may possibly grasp it in this passage from a letter, which Roosevelt revised and approved, from Owen Lattimore to Chiang Kai-shek:

Like you, the President is convinced [I suggested to the President] that for the western Pacific from about the latitude of French Indo-China to about the latitudes of Japan, the principal major powers concerned will be China and America. After this war we shall have to think of China, America, Britain and Russia as the four 'big policemen' of the world. . . . In the northern part of the Pacific, however, where American territory approaches closely to Siberia, Korea, and Japan, it would be undesirable to attempt to exclude Russia from such problems as the independence of Korea. To isolate Soviet Russia in this area of the world would run the danger of creating tension instead of relieving tension.[24]

## II. The Search for the Continental Value

### A. THE U.S. POSITION: UNIFIED ADMINISTRATION

Separate administration as well as unilateral actions by big powers were naturally incompatible with the trusteeship plan for Korea. This is clearly evident in the previously mentioned briefing-book paper for the president, which emphasized that "with the completion of military operations in Korea, there should be, so far as practicable, Allied representation in the army of occupation and in military government in Korea and that such military government should be organized on the principle of centralized administration with all of Korea administered as a single unit and not as separate zones."[25] Similarly, the American proposal entitled "Unified Administration for Korea" submitted to the Tripartite (the U.S., Great Britain, and the U.S.S.R.) Moscow Conference of Foreign Ministers, which was convened in Moscow in December 1945, also urged "a unified administration under the two military commanders acting jointly in all matters of Korean national interest" as a temporary expedient during the transitional stage until trusteeship. As a trusteeship, Korea was to be governed by "a High Commissioner and an Executive Council composed of one representative for each nation of the States composing the administrative authority."[26] These statements prove that the nonrecognition of separate administration occupied a predominant place in the U.S. policy toward Korea at this time.

The presence of such a principle challenges the view that construes the setting of the 38th parallel as an act that divided Korea between the

24. Draft of Letter from Mr. Owen Lattimore to Generalissimo Chiang Kai-shek, *FR, 1942: China,* p. 186. Bracketed revision by President Roosevelt.

25. Post-War Status of Korea, Briefing Book Paper, *FR: The Conferences at Malta and Yalta, 1945,* p. 359.

26. Memorandum by the United States Delegation at the Moscow Conference of Foreign Ministers, December 17, 1945, *FR, 1945,* vol. 2 (Washington, 1967), pp. 642–643.

U.S. and the Soviet Union, and also casts doubt on another judgment that the act was a mere product of convenience for the military. At least, in the framework of the trusteeship plan, the setting of the 38th parallel seemed rather to stem from the attempt to prevent Soviet forces from occupying all of Korea and at the same time to preserve the possibility of future joint administration by the Big Four.[27] Furthermore, there was even a desire among U.S. decision-makers for American forces alone to accept the surrender of the Japanese troops on the entire Korean peninsula. President Truman recalled, in his memoirs, that his reparation commissioner, Edwin Pauley, urged quick action in the Far East to prevent Russian excesses: "Conclusion I have reached through discussions on reparations and otherwise (I repeat otherwise) lead me to the belief that our forces should occupy quickly as much of the industrial area of Korea and Manchuria as we can, starting at the southerly tip and progressing northward."[28] Averell Harriman similarly recommended "landings be made to accept surrender of the Japanese troops at least on the Kwantung Peninsula and in Korea," because of "the way Stalin is behaving in increasing his demands on Soong."[29] Dean Rusk, one of the eyewitnesses to the drawing of the 38th parallel, testified that this line was designed to harmonize "the political desire," expressed by Secretary Byrnes, "to have U.S. forces receive the surrender as far north as possible," and "the obvious limitations on the ability of the U.S. forces to reach the area."[30]

This desire, expressed by Pauley, Harriman, and Byrnes, stemmed from growing distrust of the Soviet Union in the U.S. resulting from the events in Poland. Already by May 12, at a meeting with Grew, McCloy, and Forrestal, Harriman had requested the reexamination of the entire problem in the Far East, including the clauses in the Yalta agreement.[31] Secretary of War Stimson had also suggested to the president on the eve of the Potsdam Conference that "at least a token force of American soldiers or marines be stationed in Korea during the trusteeship," because:

The Russians, I am also informed, have already trained one or two divisions of Koreans, and, I assume, intend to use them in Korea. If an international trusteeship is not set up in Korea, and perhaps even if it is, these Korean divi-

27. See Masao Okonogi, "Beikoku no sengo Chōsen kōsō" [Postwar Korea in U.S. wartime policies], *Kokusaimondai*, No. 209, pp. 31–32.

28. Harry S. Truman, *Memoirs by Harry S. Truman: Year of Decisions* (New York, 1955), p. 433.

29. Ibid., pp. 433–434.

30. Draft Memorandum to the Joint Chiefs of Staff, *FR, 1945,* vol. 6 (Washington, 1969), p. 1039.

31. Memorandum by the Acting Secretary of State to the Secretary of the Navy (Forrestal), May 12, 1945, *FR, 1945,* vol. 7 (Washington, 1969), pp. 869–870; see also W. Averell Harriman and Elie Abel, *Special Envoy to Churchill and Stalin, 1941–1946* (New York, 1975), p. 461.

sions will probably gain control, and influence the setting up of a Soviet dominated local government, rather than an independent one. This is the Polish question transplanted to the Far East.[32]

Even in the postwar period, such distrust toward the Soviet Union was rooted in American policy in Korea. On September 29, shortly after the landing by the U.S. forces, Benninghoff, General Hodge's political advisor, foresaw in his sixth report to the secretary of state that "the United States may soon be faced with problems similar to those it faces in Rumania, Hungary and Bulgaria." Benninghoff argued that the Soviet intention in its occupational administration of North Korea was to "Sovietize."[33] Ambassador to the Soviet Union Harriman came to a similar conclusion in his report to the secretary of state on November 12: "If Soviet Government had obedient and relatively strong Korean military forces and militia which it can leave behind, it is quite possible that Soviet Govt. would be desirous of withdrawing Red army from Korea and bring pressure on us to withdraw our troops simultaneously."[34] In the light of later developments, one must recognize that this demonstrated remarkable discernment.

There still existed in Washington, however, a substantial number of officials who viewed Soviet hostility as the product of misunderstandings, and who expected that, with restraint on both sides, a mutually satisfactory resolution of differences might still occur. Such a view was actually implemented as a policy that stressed the maintenance of joint action with the Soviet Union regarding trusteeship, and self-restraint to minimize interference in the internal affairs of South Korea which might provoke the Soviet Union.[35] The Moscow Conference of Foreign Ministers held in December was considered a good opportunity to solve the question of independence for Korea. Such efforts made in Washington to resolve Soviet-American differences can often be encountered in early orders to the U.S. Headquarters in Seoul and in the secretary of state's letters.[36]

Nevertheless, what is important here is that U.S. policy at the time of the Japanese surrender did not limit itself just to the disavowal of

32. The Secretary of War (Stimson) to the President, July 10, 1945, *FR: The Conference of Berlin (The Potsdam Conference)*, vol. 2 (Washington, 1960), p. 631.

33. The Political Advisor in Korea (Benninghoff) to the Secretary of State, October 1, 1945, *FR, 1945*, vol. 6 (Washington, 1969), p. 1065.

34. The Ambassador in the Soviet Union (Harriman) to the Secretary of State, November 12, 1945, ibid., p. 1122.

35. See Masao Okonogi, "Beikoku no Chōsen seisaku niokeru reisen ninshiki no keisei, 1945–1947" [U.S. Korean Policy, 1945–1947: The formulation of the Cold War perception], *Hōgaku Kenkyū*, 50, no. 6, pp. 39–41.

36. Memorandum by the Director of the Office of Far Eastern Affairs (Vincent) to the Under Secretary of State, November 16, 1945, *FR, 1945* vol. 6, pp. 1127–1128; The Secretary of State to the Acting Political Advisor in Korea (Langdon), ibid., pp. 1137–1138.

Soviet unilateral action, but hinted as well at the possibility of taking unilateral action on its own. This implied that the distrust of the Soviet Union that originated in Europe had influenced the U.S. perception of conditions in Asia, and that the U.S. had proved its strong attachment to the realization of the axiom called self-determination. This is also suggested in the Korean case by the consensus, created in Washington by early 1946, favoring resistance to further Soviet expansion.

In May 1946, when the first Soviet-American joint commission ruptured, the U.S. began to examine the possibility of unilateral action against the Soviet Union in Korea. This indicated its recognition of the strategic value of the Korean peninsula. The document called "Policy for Korea," which was drafted by the State Department in early June with the approval of the navy and the army, gave this assessment of the strategic value of Korea:

The fundamental United States objective with regard to Korea, simply stated, is the independence of Korea. . . . Korean independence is important not only for the sake of the Koreans themselves but also as a means of strengthening political stability throughout the Far East, for the domination of Korea by either Japan or the Soviet Union would further endanger Chinese control of Manchuria and would thus lessen the prospect of the creation of a strong and stable China, without which there can be no permanent political stability in the Far East.[37]

Such a high estimate was not recorded solely in State Department documents. On May 22, Edwin Pauley, who was inspecting conditions in north and south Korea, reported:

While Korea is a small country, and in terms of our total military strength is a small responsibility, it is an ideological battleground upon which our entire success in Asia may depend. . . . Korea should receive certain needed industrial equipment from Japan as part of reparations removals. . . . [and] [t]he United States should give greater technical assistance to Korea in the reconstruction of her industrial economy.[38]

President Truman expressed his wholehearted support of such an evaluation:

Our commitments for the establishment of an independent Korea require that we stay in Korea long enough to see the job through and that we have adequate personnel and sufficient funds to do a good job.[39]

Naturally, such an evaluation did not necessarily mean U.S. adoption of a policy of unilateral action against the Soviet Union. It is important to note, however, that from this time until the proclamation of the

37. Appendix "B," Policy for Korea, FR, 1946, vol. 8 (Washington, 1971), p. 697.
38. Ambassador Edwin W. Pauley to President Truman, June 22, 1946, ibid., pp. 706, 709.
39. President Truman to Ambassador Edwin W. Pauley, July 16, 1946, ibid., p. 714.

Truman Doctrine, several temporary measures were taken: negotiations with the Soviet Union were temporarily suspended; the policy of early withdrawal of U.S. troops was repealed; 250 million in aid to south Korea for the fiscal year 1948, was examined; and there was interference in the internal affairs of south Korea to uphold a middle-of-the-road force. These all suggested that the U.S., from the summer of 1946 through the spring of 1947: (1) was still attached to a plan for the unified administration of Korea because of its commitment to the principle of self-determination; (2) placed a great deal of emphasis on Korea's strategic value in relation to the Asian continent, Manchuria, and China; and (3) regarded the Korean question as part of the larger, global relations between the U.S. and the U.S.S.R.

### B. THE SOVIET POSITION: MAINTAINING THE STATUS QUO

How did the Soviet Union seek to deal with the huge vacuum of power that emerged in northeast Asia? Since no Soviet diplomatic documents are declassified, it is difficult to answer this question. However, given its policy in eastern Europe, its postwar policy in the Far East was obviously based on the establishment of regimes around its eastern frontier contributive to its own security. In this sense, Korea, in addition to Manchuria, occupied a key position. This can be easily understood when one recalls that the center of the Russian Far East, Vladivostok, is located only seventy miles from the Korean border and is across from one of north Korea's ports, Ch'ŏngjin, which has potential as a base in the event of a sea attack on Vladivostok.[40]

Beneath this inference there lies the assumption that, even in northeast Asia, "the Russians tended to think of security in terms of space."[41] Therefore, it was historically imperative, in this respect, for Manchuria and Korea to become Soviet targets in its "defensive expansion," since prior to World War II, despite its traditional Eurocentric strategy, the Soviet Union was concerned about the possibility of Japan penetrating the continent, and therefore regarded Manchuria and Korea as a springboard for a Japanese attack on the Soviet Union. With this in mind, it is notable that R. Y. Malinowski stated in February 1946 that it was not desirable for northeast China to become an anti-Soviet base again.[42] Similarly, T. F. Shtykov stressed at the opening session of the Soviet-

---

40. This was apparent to George Kennan when U.S. forces were going to cross the 38th parallel. He said, "Obviously, they [Russians] are not going to leave the field free for us to sweep up the peninsula and place ourselves forty or fifty miles from Vladivostok." His anxieties were heightened by the difficulty he experienced in getting any satisfactory explanations from the Pentagon about U.S. bombing of the port of Najin on the east coast of north Korea. George F. Kennan, *Memoirs,* vol. II, p. 24.

41. Gaddis, *Russia, the Soviet Union and the United States,* p. 176.

42. Chiang Kai-shek, *Su-ê tsai Chung-kuo* (Taipei: 1956), p. 152.

American joint commission in March that the Soviet Union expected Korea not to be rendered a fortress or base that could be used to attack the Soviet Union in the future.[43]

Moreover, among the most significant Soviet rights recognized at Yalta related to the Far East were those concerning Manchuria, such as, the safeguard of its "preeminent interests" in the commercial port of Dairen, its lease of Port Arthur as a naval base, and the establishment of a joint Soviet-Chinese Company to operate the Chinese-Eastern Railroad and the South-Manchurian Railroad.[44] It is only natural, as the historic precedent of the Russo-Japanese War proved, that the Soviet Union would consider influence in the northern part of the Korean peninsula a prerequisite for the protection of these rights.

A natural consequence of this inference is that the major Soviet goal in northeast Asia was to prevent any opponent power from extending its influence into Manchuria and north Korea. The Soviet Union, as well as the United States, evaluated the strategic worth of the Korean peninsula in relation to the Asian continent. However, if the evaluation of the peninsula was made from similar points of view, there existed clear differences in position between the U.S. and the Soviet Union, for while the U.S. adhered to the unified administration of all Korea, the Soviet Union could achieve its previously mentioned goal by maintaining a separate occupation of Korea and severing a pro-Soviet north Korea from the southern half.

The Soviet posture of maintaining the status quo was deducible from its practical attitude toward Korea. Soviet support for a trusteeship for Korea, although it was continually expressed both during and after the war, should not be taken literally. Rather, the Soviet Union, as its interests in the Far East became well defined, was gradually compelled to reveal its reluctance to accept a unified administration and trusteeship that gave it only one-quarter of the authority. Stalin, for example, inquired whether any foreign troops would be stationed in Korea, and replied, "The shorter the period the better," when Roosevelt discussed the twenty- to thirty-year trusteeship plan at Yalta.[45] By the same token, in reply to the U.S. proposal for the establishment of a High Commissioner, and an Executive Council composed of one representative from each nation having administrative authority, the Soviet Union, at the Moscow Conference of Foreign Ministers, demanded the establishment of a "provisional democratic government" by the Korean people themselves, and

43. *Seoul Sinmun*, March 21, 1946.
44. Agreement Regarding Entry of the Soviet Union into the War against Japan, February 11, 1945, *FR: The Conferences at Malta and Yalta*, p. 984.
45. Bohlen Minutes to the Roosevelt-Stalin Meeting, February 8, 1945, ibid., p. 770.

urged limiting the trusteeship to a five-year period.[46] Furthermore, on March 23, 1946, Stalin frankly stated to Harriman: "The Soviet government does not need a trusteeship any more than the United States. If both countries consider it desirable the trusteeship can be abolished."[47]

This attitude on the Soviet part did not change even after the joint commission was convened. Of course the Soviet government did not necessarily oppose the joint commission directly, but it persistently refused to allow the participation of right-wing forces led by Syngman Rhee and Kim Ku in discussions regarding the establishment of a government. This Soviet demand to exclude the "anti-democratic faction" was the direct cause of the ruptures of the first and second Soviet-American joint commissions, and the demand shows the limits of Soviet concessions. To the Soviet Union, the presence of U.S. troops in south Korea and the participation of right-wing forces in the provisional government under an international administration meant nothing but a road to a unified Korea under an anti-Soviet government.[48]

In the summer of 1947, when the second Soviet-American joint commission was on the verge of virtual collapse, the Soviet Union shifted its policy toward the simultaneous withdrawal of both American and Soviet troops from Korea.[49] It is doubtful that the new Soviet policy remained purely defensive, because this scheme was based on a Soviet analysis of the Korean situation in which "the progressive forces which would assume responsibility for the fate of this nation [Korea] had already emerged."[50] In addition, the Russians might have seen that the withdrawal of foreign troops would leave the north Korean–Soviet partnership in a stronger position against the troubled U.S.–south Korean one. Nevertheless, given these major aspects of Soviet policy toward Korea, it is unrealistic to perceive the Soviet proposal in September 1947 as an underplot to unify north and south Korea by force. The more rational interpretation is that the Soviet withdrawal, which began in October 1948, made the U.S. withdrawal easier, and was an attempt to resolve the Korean problem without resorting to military commitments by big powers. The net effect of withdrawal, in any case, would mean the localiza-

46. See F. I. Shabshina, "Koreja posle Vtoroj mirovoj vojny," *Krizis kolonial'no-osvoboditel'naja bor'ba narodov Vostocnoj Azii,* ed., E. M. Zhukov (Moscow, 1949).

47. Harriman and Abel, *Special Envoy,* p. 533.

48. The Political Advisor in Korea (Langdon) to the Secretary of State, October 9, 1946, *FR, 1946,* p. 744.

49. See the Statement of the Ministry of Foreign Affairs of the USSR, September 20, 1947, in *The Soviet Union and the Korean Question* (Moscow, 1948; rpt. London, 1950), pp. 61–62.

50. E. M. Zhukov, ed., *Meždunarodnye otnošeija na dal'nem vostoke 1890–1949* (Moscow: 1956), p. 693.

tion of the conflict, and an increase in Soviet influence in the Korean peninsula.[51]

On the other hand, the Soviet government seemed adamant in its efforts to establish a strong pro-Soviet regime in the northern half of the peninsula. As early as October 13, 1945, the north Korean communist organization was cut off from the Korean communists in Seoul, and on October 17 Kim Il Sung took charge of it. In conjunction with this, on February 8, 1946, the legislative assembly, which had been primarily composed of nationalists and old communists, was taken over by a Provisional People's Committee for North Korea headed by Kim Il Sung, which immediately undertook a "program of democratic reformation," including land reform. This took place about two weeks before the first meeting of the Soviet-American joint commission.[52]

The consolidation of north Korean independence progressed steadily as the joint commission stagnated, and by August two left-wing parties had merged to form the North Korean Workers' Party. In February of 1947 the North Korean People's Assembly and the North Korean People's Committee were formally inaugurated through a general election. In this way, by the spring of 1947 north Korea had already attained a state system similar to those generally seen in communist nations, that is, party-government–people's assembly.[53] It was this consolidation of the pro-Soviet regime that laid the foundation for the firm Soviet posture at the second joint commission meeting, and that made possible the proposal for early withdrawal of American and Soviet troops.

### III. The U.S. Withdrawal from Korea

#### A. THE FIRST STAGE: THE PERIPHERY IN THE WORLD

U.S. policy toward Korea in 1946 might be described as a part of its larger global policy, and was reflected by "a noticeable toughening of United States policy toward the Soviet Union" during the spring and the summer of that year.[54] This policy remained in effect until early 1947. On February 15, 1947, the Special Inter-Departmental Committee on Korea, which was established to prepare recommendations for the secretaries, adopted in a draft report "a properly planned, aggressive approach" to the Soviet Union. The committee requested that the president forward to

51. See Okonogi, "The Domestic Roots of the Korean War," p. 311.

52. See Dae-Sook Suh, *The Korean Communist Movement, 1918–1948* (Princeton, N.J., 1967), pp. 319–320; Kim Nam-sik, *Sillok Namnodang* [The true record of the Workers' Party of south Korea] (Seoul: 1975), pp. 49–61.

53. See Pang In-hu, *Puk'han "Chosŏn Nodongdang" ŭi hyŏngsŏng kwa paljŏn* [The formation and development of the "Workers' Party of Korea" in north Korea] (Seoul, 1967), p. 102.

54. Gaddis, *Russia, the Soviet Union and the United States,* pp. 183–184.

Congress draft legislation for a "grant-in-aid" to Korea of 250 million for various projects during fiscal 1948.[55] Yet, this report was made without precise assessments of whether the means existed to carry them out.[56] Accordingly, with the proclamation of the Truman Doctrine on March 12, 1947, U.S. commitments had to be reorganized in the framework of the new strategy, with priority given to Europe. Syngman Rhee, then conducting personal diplomacy in the United States, sent the president a note which emphasized that "Korea is located in a strategic situation similar to that of Greece and the Korean patriots are greatly encouraged in their fight for freedom by your inspiring message."[57] By then, the focal issue was whether Korea would become the Greece of the Far East.

A shift in the strategic appraisal of Korea was already noticeable in an April 4 letter from Secretary of War Patterson to Secretary of State Marshall: "The apparent inability of the U.S. to carry out its policies in Korea may have some impact on the Japanese people and on U.S. security interests in the Far East. . . . [L]ogically the policy concerning Korea must be viewed as part of an integrated whole which includes Manchuria and China." He also stressed that, based on the equivalent strengths of the respective occupation forces, Korea was the most problematic occupation area, and that, from the standpoint of U.S. security, the probabilities of long-term benefits were low.[58] Furthermore, Patterson was convinced of the seriousness of the situation when he said: "The United States should pursue forcefully a course of action whereby we get out of Korea at an early data. . . . All our measures should have early withdrawal as their overriding objective." He feared that the proposal to ask Congress to authorize a 540-million aid program for the next three years would "occasion an adverse reaction resulting in a net reduction of the funds provided to the War Department and other agencies for support of U.S. policy throughout the world."

A similar line of reasoning can also be observed in a report by the Joint Strategic Survey Committee dated April 29, which declared: "This is the one country within which we alone have for almost two years carried on ideological warfare in direct contact with our opponents, so that to lose this battle would be gravely detrimental to United States prestige, and therefore security, throughout the world." In this report, Korea, although fourth, next to Greece, Italy, and Iran, among the fifteen nations

55. Memorandum by the Special Inter-Departmental Committee on Korea, February 25, 1947, *FR, 1947,* vol. 6 (Washington, 1972), p. 609.

56. Gaddis, *Russia, the Soviet Union and the United States,* p. 184.

57. Dr. Syngman Rhee to President Truman, March 13, 1947, *FR, 1947,* vol. 6, p. 620.

58. The Secretary of War (Patterson) to the Acting Secretary of State, April 4, 1947, ibid., pp. 626–627.

that it was desirable to aid "because of their need," ranked next to last in a ranking of nations that it was desirable to aid "because of their importance to the national security of the United States." Eventually, while Greece acquired fifth place next to Italy, Korea was ranked thirteenth out of sixteen nations in the preferential order of American foreign aid.[59]

Under these circumstances, when the second Soviet-American joint commission broke up in early July 1947, U.S. policy toward Korea reached a climactic turning point. The reexamination of the policy was made by three groups: the Ad Hoc Committee on Korea, a subcommittee of the State-War-Navy Coordinating Committee (SWNCC); the Wedemeyer Mission that was dispatched to China and Korea in mid-July; and the Joint Chiefs of Staff, which analyzed the interest of the United States in the military occupation of south Korea from the point of view of the military security of the U.S.[60]

Above all, the conclusion reached by the Joint Chiefs of Staff was particularly distinct because it was not concerned with political considerations. Its view, as contained in Secretary of Defense Forrestal's memorandum of September 29, was that the United States had little strategic interest in maintaining the present troops and bases in Korea. Three reasons were given for this view.[61]

[1] In the event of hostilities in the Far East, our present forces in Korea would be a military liability and could not be maintained there without substantial reinforcement prior to the initiation of hostilities. . . .
[2] In the light of the present severe shortage of military manpower, the corps of two divisions, totaling some 45,000 men, now maintained in south Korea, could well be used elsewhere. . . .
[3] At the present time, the occupation of Korea is requiring very large expenditures for the primary purpose of preventing disease and disorder. . . .

Compared to this, the other two groups, while approving U.S. withdrawal from Korea in principle, were still deeply concerned with the maintenance of United States prestige. The Wedemeyer report, for example, asserted that "A withdrawal of all American assistance . . . would cost the United States an immense loss in moral prestige among the people of Asia." Similarly, SWNCC 176–30 insisted:

The U.S. cannot at this time withdraw from Korea under circumstances which would inevitably lead to Communist domination of the entire country. The re-

59. United States Assistance to Other Countries from the Standpoint of National Security, Report by the Joint Strategic Survey Committee, April 29, 1947, *FR, 1947,* vol. 1 (Washington, 1973), pp. 737–738, 744.
60. See Okonogi, "Beikoku no Chōsen seisaku. . . ," p. 48.
61. Memorandum by the Secretary of Defense (Forrestal) to the Secretary of State, September 26 [29], 1947, *FR, 1947,* vol. 6, pp. 817–818.

sulting political repercussions would seriously damage U.S. prestige in the Far East and throughout the world, and would discourage those small nations now relying upon the U.S. to support them in resisting internal or external Communist pressure.[62]

After these proposals had been considered, U.S. policy was decided on September 29. The new policy was to oppose the Soviet proposal for the simultaneous withdrawal of U.S. and Soviet occupation forces from Korea, and to support presenting the Korean problem to the United Nations. This was clearly not a decision for U.S. withdrawal from Korea. However, in making this decision, Marshall, Lovett, Kennan, Butterworth, Rusk, and Allison agreed on the following important points: (1) ultimately the U.S. position in Korea was untenable even with the expenditure of considerable U.S. money and effort; (2) the U.S., however, could not "scuttle" and run from Korea without considerable loss of prestige and political standing in the Far East and in the world at large; and (3) it should be the effort of the government through all proper means to effect a settlement of the Korean problem which would enable the U.S. to withdraw from Korea as soon as possible with a minimum of bad effects.[63] All these conclusions were adopted intact by the National Security Council a half year later when it decided to withdraw U.S. troops.

Undeniably, 1947 was a turning point in American policy toward Korea. The U.S. did not intend to ignore the prestige she had staked on the freedom and independence of Korea, but was compelled to give precedence to withdrawal from south Korea. Withdrawal caused a fundamental transformation in American policy from joint action to unilateral action, from the unified administration of Korea to the establishment of an independent south Korean government, and from support of a middle-of-the-road force to the buttressing of the right wing.[64] Moreover, this shift in U.S. policy entailed a basic modification in the appraisal of Korea's strategic value. For the first time since the Second World War, the U.S. abandoned the unification of Korea and ceased to evaluate Korea's strategic value in terms of the Asian continent. Moreover, it is important to reiterate that the withdrawal from Korea was attributed to its peripheral character at the global level. Observed from this angle, it was a direct product of the asymmetric development of the cold war between Europe and Asia that began with the Truman Doctrine.

62. Report to the President on China-Korea, September 1947, Submitted by Lieutenant General H. L. Wedemeyer, ibid., p. 803; SWNCC 176-30, Report by the Ad Hoc Committee on Korea, August 4, 1947, ibid., p. 738.
63. Memorandum by the Director of the Office of Far Eastern Affairs (Butterworth) to the Under Secretary of State (Lovett), October 1, 1947, ibid., p. 820.
64. See Okonogi, "Beikoku no Chōsen seisaku. . . ," pp. 51–52.

B. THE SECOND STAGE: THE PERIPHERY IN THE FAR EAST

The conclusion to withdraw from Korea in no way implied that the U.S. had built up a systematic strategy for East Asia at that time. Admittedly, the U.S. seemed to consider Japan proper of greater weight than the Asian continent after the spring of 1947. However, only after two reports by the Policy Planning Staff appeared in October and November did the U.S. modify its occupation policy in Japan to bring it in line with its strategy against the Soviet Union. Moreover, while these reports urged that "our policy must be directed toward restoring a balance of power in Europe and Asia," the primary instrument of containment was still limited to producing "the political and economic stability which Japanese society would require if it was to withstand communist pressure after we had gone."[65]

It was not until 1948 that the anti-Soviet strategy in East Asia was formulated in military terms. A Policy Planning Staff report—PPS 23—dated February 24, which George Kennan called "a first step toward the unified concept of foreign policy," stated, "We should make a careful study to see what parts of the Pacific and Far Eastern world are absolutely vital to our security, and we should concentrate our policy on seeing to it that those areas remain in hands which we can control or rely on." In addition, Kennan noted that, "Japan and the Philippines will be found to be the corner-stones of such a Pacific security system."[66]

Kennan, who visited Tokyo immediately after presenting PPS 23 to the secretary and the under secretary of state, succeeded in consulting with MacArthur on this problem. The "most desirable political-strategic concept for the western Pacific area" was clearly defined in a March 14 letter from Kennan to Marshal:

1. While we should endeavor to influence events on the mainland of Asia in ways favorable to our security, we would not regard any mainland areas as vital to us. Korea would accordingly be evacuated as soon as possible.
2. Okinawa would be made the center of our offensive striking power in the western Pacific area. It would constitute the central and most advanced point of a U-shaped U.S. security zone embracing the Aleutians, the

65. PPS-10, Memorandum by the Director of the Policy Planning Staff (Kennan), Results of Planning Staff Study of Questions Involved in the Japanese Peace Settlement, October 14, 1947, ibid., pp. 537–543; PPS-13, Report by the Policy Planning Staff, Resume of World Situation, November 6, 1947, *FR, 1947,* vol. 1 (Washington, 1973), pp. 770–777. The quotes are from the latter source, pp. 771, 775.

66. Memorandum by the Director of the Policy Planning Staff (Kennan) to the Secretary of State and the Under Secretary of State (Lovett), February 24, 1948, *FR, 1948,* vol. 1, pt. 2 (Washington, 1976), p. 509; PPS-23, Report by the Policy Planning Staff, Review of Current Trends in U.S. Foreign Policy, February 24, 1948, ibid., p. 525.

Ryukyus, the former Japanese mandated islands, and of course Guam. We would then rely on Okinawa-based air power, plus our advance naval power, to prevent the assembling and launching [of] any amphibious force from any mainland port in the east-central or northeast Asia.

3. Japan and the Philippines would remain outside this security area, and we would not attempt to keep bases or forces on their territory, *provided* that they remained entirely demilitarized and that no other power made any effort to obtain strategic facilities on them. They would thus remain neutralized areas, enjoying complete political independence, situated on the immediate flank of our security zone.[67]

In this way, the U.S. withdrawal from Korea came to be related to the new strategy for East Asia. Furthermore, being a confirmation of the decision made the previous fall, it needed no elaboration. As Kennan expected, the National Security Council (NSC), after deliberating over a report submitted by the State-Army-Navy-Air Force Coordinating Committee (SANACC), gave the president its recommendation—NSC 8—advising him that "it should be the effort of the U.S. Government through all proper means to effect a settlement of the Korean problem which would enable the U.S. to withdraw from Korea as soon as possible with the minimum of bad effects."[68] This recommendation was approved by the president on April 8, and was promptly sent to the U.S. Headquarters in Seoul. The withdrawal was scheduled to be completed by December 31.

In addition, NSC 8 called for the "expeditious completion of existing plans for expanding, training, and equipping the south Korean constabulary as a means of providing, so far as practicable, effective protection for the security of south Korea against any but an overt act of aggression by north Korea or other forces" before withdrawing. However, there was no definite military plan on what to do if there was an "overt act of aggression." This paper makes a point that Dean Acheson also made in his famous National Press Club speech:

The overthrow by Soviet-dominated forces of a regime established in south Korea under the aegis of the UN would, moreover, constitute a severe blow to the prestige and influence of the UN; in this respect the interests of the U.S. are parallel to, if not identical with, those of the UN.[69]

Another remarkable feature of the new East Asia strategy was that Korea was hardly linked to Japanese security. As mentioned previously,

67. The Director of the Policy Planning Staff (Kennan) to the Secretary of State, March 14, 1948, ibid., p. 534.
68. NSC 8, Report by the National Security Council on the Position of the United States with Respect to Korea, April 2, 1948, *FR, 1948,* vol. 6 (Washington, 1974), p. 1168.
69. Ibid., pp. 1167–1169.

the new strategy was based on the maintenance of a demilitarized Japan whose security was dependent on other regions. However, neither Kennan nor MacArthur was inclined to assure Japan's security by the continuation of an American commitment to south Korea. Instead, they sought to rely on the naval facilities and air power existing in the western Pacific. Okinawa was the most advanced and vital point in this structure. MacArthur assumed that by maintaining naval and air bases in Okinawa, the U.S. could "easily control every one of the ports of northern Asia from which an amphibious operation could conceivably be launched."[70]

Nonetheless, as the day for withdrawal drew closer, it was inevitable that a thorough study on the amphibious character of the Korean peninsula would be made from a standpoint different from MacArthur's and Kennan's. This alternate view was presented by Bishop, Chief of the Division of Northeast Asian Affairs, who argued that "the question of withdrawal from Korea must be linked to the larger question of the probable repercussions of such withdrawal throughout northeast Asia on the national objectives and the security position of the United States in the Pacific area." Bishop went further and added:

Should communist domination of the entire Korean peninsula become an accomplished fact, the islands of Japan would be surrounded on three sides by an unbroken arc of communist territories with the extremities of the Japanese archipelago virtually within gunshot range of Soviet positions in Sakhalin and the Kuriles in the northeast and communist positions in southern Korea in the Southwest.[71]

Certainly, NSC 8 did touch on this point more or less. The extension of Soviet control over all of Korea, according to this document, "would enhance the political strategic position of the Soviet Union with respect to both China and Japan, and adversely affect the position of the U.S. in those areas and throughout the Far East." The problem, as mentioned above, was how to cope with "an overt act of aggression."

Eventually, Bishop's demand to reexamine NSC 8 was adopted by Butterworth, and after informal discussions of this subject between officials of the Department of the Army and the Department of State, a jointly prepared message was sent to MacArthur to obtain his view with respect to the overall impact of early troop withdrawal from Korea, particularly as it affected the U.S. position in Japan.[72] MacArthur replied

70. Conversation between General of the Army MacArthur and Mr. George F. Kennan, March 5, 1948, ibid., p. 701.

71. Draft Memorandum Submitted to the Director of the Office of Far Eastern Affairs (Butterworth), ibid., p. 1338.

72. Memorandum by the Director of Far Eastern Affairs (Butterworth) to the Acting Secretary of State, January 10, 1949, FR, 1949, vol. 7, pt. 2 (Washington, 1976), pp. 942–943; The Secretary of the Army (Royall) to the Secretary of State, January 25, 1949, ibid., p. 945.

that the United States did not have the capability to train and equip Korean troops to the point where the Koreans would be able to cope with a full-scale invasion accompanied by internal disturbances caused by the communists, and that if a serious threat developed, the United States would have to give up active military support of ROK forces.[73] He added, "The longer U.S. forces remain in Korea the greater [the] risk of being placed in position of effecting withdrawal under conditions amounting to direct pressure rather than as a voluntary act."[74] In conclusion, MacArthur recommended that the American withdrawal should terminate on May 10, the first anniversary of the general election in south Korea. This recommendation undoubtedly had a great deal of influence on the debate in the National Security Council on March 22. As a result of this meeting, the National Security Council submitted to the President NSC 8-2, which set June 30 as the terminal date for withdrawal; it was approved by the president the next day.[75]

## IV. The Amphibious Power Vacuum: A Different Evaluation

One of the main objectives in the concept of containment worked out by the Policy Planning Staff in 1947 and 1948 was to "negotiate mutual withdrawal of Soviet and American forces from the advanced positions they had occupied since the end of World War II."[76] This concept was the basis for the previously mentioned strategy to depend, as far as Japan's security was concerned, on the military bases in the Western Pacific, especially Okinawa. The concept also led to the view, with regard to a peace treaty with Japan, that "we should . . . seek through the diplomatic channel the concurrence of a majority of the participating countries in the principal points of content."[77] As a result, both NSC 13-2 of October 1948 and NSC 13-3 of May 1949 recommended that "the numbers of tactical, and especially non-tactical, forces should be minimized" in Japan even during the pretreaty period.[78]

However, the Joint Chiefs of Staff, affected by the extremely critical situation in China during the spring and summer of 1949, were gravely concerned about this external threat, and gradually moved to evaluate

73. Robert K. Sawyer, *Military Advisors in Korea: KMAG in Peace and War* (Washington, 1962), p. 37.

74. The Secretary of the Army (Royall) to the Secretary of State, January 25, 1949, *FR, 1949,* vol. 7, p. 946.

75. NSC 8-2, Report by the National Security Council to the President, Position of the United States with Respect to Korea, March 22, 1949, ibid., pp. 969–978.

76. Gaddis, *Russia, the Soviet Union and the United States,* p. 193.

77. NSC 13-2, Report by the National Security Council on Recommendations with Respect to United States Policy toward Japan, October 7, 1948, *FR, 1948,* vol. 6, p. 858.

78. Ibid., p. 859; NSC 13-3, Report by the National Security Council on Recommendations with Respect to United States Policy toward Japan, May 6, 1949, *FR, 1949,* vol. 7, pt. 2, p. 731.

Japan's value in terms of military strategy and to prolong the occupation of Japan. The document referring to Japan's limited rearmament, which the Joint Chiefs of Staff submitted to the National Security Council on June 15, argued:

Commensurate with the degree to which Japanese western orientation is maintained, Japan's capacity for self-defense must be developed against the time when it may be determined by the Soviets that overt aggression by them or their satellites is their only means for gaining control over Japan.[79]

It also modified the strategy of Kennan and MacArthur in that Japan was now to be embraced as a major portion of "the defensive perimeter":

The ultimate minimum United States position in the Far East vis-a-vis the USSR, one to which we are rapidly being forced, requires at least our present degree of control of the Asian offshore island chain. In the event of war, this island chain should constitute in effect a system of strong outposts for our strategic position. It would have only limited offensive value, however, and might well be untenable, if any major portion of the chain, such as Japan, were unavailable at the outset of the struggle.[80]

On the other hand, the State Department sought to modify NSC 13-2 and 13-3 in a direction different from that proposed by the Joint Chiefs of Staff. As reported by George Kennan, Dean Acheson had reached the conclusion by the fall of 1949 that "it was both desirable and urgent to press for early conclusion of a treaty of peace with Japan regardless of objections of the Russians and, if necessary, without their consent."[81] In fact at a conference with British Foreign Minister Ernest Bevin on September 17, Acheson said that

we [the U.S.] were in favor of working out a Treaty soon, that our interests were so great in Japan that we could not get ourselves in a position in which we had to approve a treaty we did not like, or in which our failure to approve would result in a treaty going into effect without our consent.[82]

Also, a Department of State critique of the position taken by the Joint Chiefs was submitted to the National Security Council on September 30. This critique stressed the necessity of an early peace treaty.

The only hope for the preservation and advancement of such democracy and western orientation as now exists in Japan lies in the early conclusion of a

79. NSC 49, Report by the Joint Chief of Staff, Strategic Evaluation of United States Security Needs in Japan, June 9, 1949, ibid., p. 776.
    80. Ibid., pp. 774–775.
    81. George F. Kennan, *Memoirs,* vol. 2, pp. 40–41.
    82. Memorandum of Conversation by the Secretary of State, September 17, 1949, *FR, 1949,* vol. 7, pt. 2, p. 861.

peace settlement with that country. From the political point of view, the achievement of our objectives with respect to Japan are now less likely to be thwarted by proceeding promptly to a peace treaty than by continuance of the occupation regime, provided that essential U.S. military needs in Japan are assured in the treaty or other concurrent arrangements.[83]

These new policies prepared by the Joint Chiefs of Staff and the State Department were adjusted at the end of 1949 and early in 1950 toward the early conclusion of a peace treaty to meet the demands of military strategy. For example, a paper prepared by the staff of the National Security Council and presented to that body on December 23, 1949 defined the Asian offshore island chain as "our first line of defense, and, in addition, our first line of offense from which we may seek to reduce the area of Communist control"[84] On January 12, Acheson, referring to the "defensive perimeter" described in this paper, explained:

The defeat and disarmament of Japan has placed upon the United States the necessity of assuming the military defense of Japan so long as that is required, both in the interest of our security and, in all honor, in the interest of Japanese security. . . . I can assure you that there is no intention of any sort of abandoning or weakening the defenses of Japan and that whatever arrangements are to be made either through permanent settlement or otherwise, that defense must and shall be maintained.[85]

There was another significant movement under way in northeast Asia in late 1949, that is, the militarization of north Korea. The north Korean People's Army was officially activated on February 8, 1948. Its first full infantry divisions, the 3rd and 4th, were established between 1947 and 1949, and its first armored unit, the 105th Armored Battalion, was established in October 1948.[86] Only after the summer of 1949, however, were the north Korean forces reinforced to the extent that a large-scale invasion of the south, such as that of June 1950, could be carried out. This reinforcement came from two sources: the return of nearly 50,000 Korean volunteers from China, and the transport of large quantities of heavy arms and T34 tanks from Vladivostok to Ch'ŏngjin in the spring of 1950.

83. NSC 49-1, Department of State Comments on NSC 49, September 30, 1949, ibid., pp. 872–873. On NSC 49 series, see editors' headnote in Thomas Etzold and John Gaddis eds., *Containment: Documents on American Policy and Strategy, 1945–1950* (New York, 1978), p. 230.

84. Etzold and Gaddis, *Containment,* p. 264. See editors' headnote on NSC 48 series, p. 251.

85. "Crisis in Asia—An Examination of U.S. Policy," *The Department of State Bulletin* 22, no. 551 (January 23, 1950):115–116. This article is the text of the speech Acheson delivered to the National Press Club on January 12.

86. Roy E. Appleman, *United States Army in the Korean War: South to the Naktong, North to the Yalu* (Washington, 1961), p. 9.

As for the former, as early as July 1949 it was known that Korean soldiers who had served in the 164th and 166th Divisions of the Chinese Communist Forces had been incorporated into the 5th and 6th Divisions, respectively, of the north Korean army. In addition, early in April 1950 about 12,000 men drawn from the Chinese communist 139th, 140th, 141st, and 156th divisions were moved by rail to north Korea, where they were reorganized into the north Korean 7th Division. In addition to these three divisions, the north Korean 1st and 4th Divisions each had one regiment of veterans from the Chinese Communist Forces. Consequently, Korean veterans from the Chinese Communist Forces made up about one-third of the entire north Korean regular army, which consisted of 135,000 men.[87]

With respect to the latter, the Soviet supply of modern weapons was reflected by a movement in north Korea seeking donations for the purchase of arms. This movement was extensively promoted after mid-October to procure planes, tanks, and ships. Its core was the Association of Supporters for Protecting and Defending the Fatherland, which had been established on July 15, and for which 3 million members were mobilized by the spring of the following year.[88] A ceremony for the presentation of funds donated was held at the People's Army Art Theater on January 25, 1950.[89] In addition to this fund-raising campaign, the 105th Armored Battalion, which was established in October 1948, was increased to regimental strength by May 1949, and had become an Armored Brigade with a strength of 6,000 men and 120 tanks by June 1950.[90]

Apart from these, there were specific indications that north Korea was becoming a military base. Partisan activities in south Korea, for example, were transformed by the penetration of partisans from a guerrilla base in north Korea after June 28, 1949, when the Democratic Front for the Unification of the Fatherland was formed. The guerrilla squads were sent across the 38th parallel in ten different waves, and by the spring of 1950 they were estimated to number appoximately 2,000 men.[91] An article in *Pravda* dated March 27, 1950, in which Pak Hŏn-yŏng, vice-chairman of the Korean Workers' Party, discussed the heroic struggle by the south Korean people, stated that the immediate problem for the com-

87. Ibid., pp. 9–10.
88. Wire service from the Korean Central News Agency to Construction News Agency in Tokyo, January 4, 1950.
89. Ibid., January 25, 1950.
90. Appleman, *United States Army in the Korean War,* p. 10.
91. On partisan activities in South Korea, see Kim, *Sillok Namnodang,* and Kim Chŏmgon, *Han'guk chŏnjaeng kwa Nodongdang chŏllyak* [The Korean War and the strategy of the Workers' Party] (Seoul: 1973).

munists was to combine "democratic construction" in north Korea and "armed struggle" in south Korea.[92]

Such activities incontestably reflected a change in the Soviet policy toward north Korea. Of these three initiatives, the gathering of donations was undoubtedly based on a prior Soviet decision to supply north Korean troops with a large volume of the latest weapons. Given the trend in relations between the Soviet Union and north Korea during this period, it is also difficult to believe that the return of the Korean volunteers from the Chinese Communist Forces, and their subsequent assignment to the north Korean Army, had nothing to do with the Soviet policy of reinforcing the north Korean Army. The dispatch of guerrilla bands to the south is more difficult to evaluate. However, in view of the fact that, in late 1949 and early 1950, the Soviet Union praised guerrilla activities in south Korea, and that the initiation of guerrilla activities coincided with a Soviet reexamination of Asian people's liberation movements following the Chinese revolution, we may surmise that the Soviet Union was favorably disposed toward south Korean guerrilla activity.

It was clearly demonstrated, even in statements by north Korean leaders, that a new role was imposed upon north Korea after the summer of 1949. In March 1948, Kim Il Sung defined the northern half of the Korean peninsula as "headquarters for democratic forces which would save the homeland from the American imperialists' policy of colonial subordination," but it was necessary to redefine it as "a steadfast fortress with enough power to secure the unification and the integration of the homeland" in September 1949.[93] Moreover, in his New Year's message for 1950, this new definition was clarified; north Korea was a "new headquarters to guarantee a democratic victory for the patriots who rose up in the struggle for the unification of the homeland."[94] This statement was made concurrently with a speech given by Minister of National Defense Ch'oe Yong-gŏn at the same ceremony for the presentation of funds donated to purchase arms. Ch'oe stated:

The Korean People's Army, succeeding to the indomitable spirit and tradition of the partisan corps, which was organized by the distinguished sons and daughters of our homeland under the leadership of Premier Kim Il Sung, the peerless patriot of our people, has thoroughly prepared itself for a mobilization, which the people of our land might demand at any time and any place, by training itself in military technique and consolidating its armaments.[95]

92. Pak Hŏn-yŏng, "The heroic struggles of the South Korean people for the unification and independence of the fatherland," *Pravda*, March 27, 1950.

93. Kim's address to the second congress of the Korean Workers' Party, in *Kin Nissei Senshu*, supplement (Tokyo, 1952), p. 35; ibid., p. 178.

94. Korean Central News Agency, January 1, 1950.

95. Ibid., January 26, 1950.

Up until the outbreak of the Korean War on June 25, 1950, such movement by the communists was hardly recognized. Even after the war began, there was a failure to grasp precisely the Soviet intentions behind it, owing to an absorption in the surprise attack by the north Korean Army. However, in retrospect, this movement clearly corresponded to a new movement in Japan. North Korea must have meant more to the Soviet Union than did Japan to the U.S. This was clearly illustrated by two events that happened in the Far East in early 1950.

The first of these was the criticism of the Japanese Communist Party by the Cominform. This criticism began abruptly with an article that appeared in the January 6 issue of the *Cominform Journal,* and that was signed "Observer." This article severely condemned the situation in Japan.

They should wage a resolute struggle for the independence of Japan, for the establishment of a democratic and peace-loving Japan, for the immediate conclusion of a just peace treaty, for the speedy withdrawal of American troops from Japan and to ensure lasting peace between the people.[96]

It was quite apparent that this demand resulted from a strong consciousness of American policy toward Japan since the previous fall, because the article began by analyzing American policy in the following manner:

After the failure of the predatory plans of American imperialists in China and Korea, the State Department and U.S. militarists focussed their main attention on Japan as the principal base for military ventures against the Soviet Union and the democratic movement in the countries of Asia. Above all, they try, by means of various groundless pretexts, to delay the signing of a peace treaty with Japan, and, in this way, to legalize a long term stay of the American army there.

The second event indicating the Soviet Union's interest in north Korea was the conclusion, on February 14, of the Sino-Soviet Treaty of Friendship, Alliance, and Mutual Assistance. In the first article of this treaty, the two parties declared they would take joint action "for the purpose of preventing aggressive action on the part of Japan or any other state which should unite with Japan, directly or indirectly, in aggressive actions."[97] They also pledged in the second article to make efforts to conclude a peace treaty with Japan as soon as this was possible. This alliance, according to the *People's Daily,* implied the formation of a coalition between continental nations that was designed to cope with the military alliance between the U.S. and Japan.

96. *For a Lasting Peace, for a People's Democracy!,* January 6, 1950.
97. Nihon Kokusai Mondai Kenkyu Sho [Japan Institute for International Affairs] ed., *Shin Chūgoku shiryō shūsei* [Collected materials on new China], vol. 3, (Tokyo, 1969), pp. 54–55.

Established in a new era in history, this alliance between China and the Soviet Union embraces one-third of the world's population. The Alliance is an unconquerable bastion against imperialist invasion. This will effectively prevent Japan, or any other country directly or indirectly entering into an alliance with her, from again committing aggression and destroying world peace. Therefore, this alliance is a severe attack on American imperialism, which is even now attempting to revive Japanese aggression.[98]

In view of the basic direction in Soviet policy in the Far East that was demonstrated by these two events, it can be presumed that the southward advance by the north Korea in June 1950 was, for the Soviets, a type of "defensive expansion" prosecuted in the form of "civil war." The Soviet Union wanted to fill the amphibious power vacuum that had appeared during the previous summer for two reasons. First, such a move would prevent the military concert between the U.S. and Japan from spreading to south Korea; second, the move would have a serious impact, politically, socially, and psychologically, on Japan and would stimulate elements in Japan favoring a neutral course.[99] Of these, the former was in line with the purpose of the newly established Sino-Soviet alliance, and the latter was compatible with criticism of the Japanese Communist Party by the Cominform.

On the other hand, American policy toward Korea did not change even after the summer of 1949, partly because of its underestimation of the north Korean army's capability, and also because of its optimistic miscalculation of Soviet intentions. MacArthur, who played a great role in the withdrawal of the U.S. troops from Korea, changed his view, after the summer of 1949, by endorsing the long-term maintenance of U.S. navy and air bases in Japan.[100] Nevertheless, he was not convinced that the militarization of Japan would trigger a southward advance by the north Korean army. He clarified his position in a statement to the Huber Congressional Committee while it was in Tokyo in September 1949: "As long as south Korea is not a threat to north Korea no action will be taken by the Kremlin to absorb it as there would be nothing to gain by taking it over."[101]

However, the basic reason the U.S. did not change its attitude toward Korea may be found in its Far Eastern strategy itself. As already noted, the paper presented to the National Security Council by the Joint

98. *Jen-min jih-pao,* February 16, 1950.

99. See Marshall D. Shulman, *Stalin's Foreign Policy,* pp. 142–144.

100. Memorandum of Conversation, by the Acting Political Advisor in Japan (Sebald), September 21, 1949, *FR, 1949,* vol. 7 (Washington, 1976), pp. 862–864; Memorandum of Conversation, by Mr. Robert A. Fearey, of the Office of Northeast Asian Affairs, November 2, 1949, ibid., pp. 890–894.

101. Memorandum of Conversation, by Mr. Allen B. Moreland, Department of State Representative with the Huber Congressional Committee on Far Eastern Tour, September 5, 1949, *FR, 1949,* vol. 9 (Washington, 1974), p. 546.

Chiefs of Staff in June 1949 had requested the limited rearmament of Japan to protect that country from the danger of external attack. Nonetheless, militarization of south Korea was not required for the "defensive perimeter" strategy that used the Asian offshore island chain as the first line for American security. Moreover, as Major General Charles Bolte testified at the hearings of the House Committee on Foreign Affairs in the summer of 1949, MacArthur would prefer to lose Pusan to the Soviets rather than fight there himself, because, "Our air bases [in Japan] are well within range of any of those points, sufficiently to deny them the use of it."[102] From this point of view not only was the militarization of south Korea not essential for the "defensive perimeter," its abandonment was also strategically justified.

### Conclusion

Emerging as a major power in the post-Pearl Harbor Asian-Pacific region, the United States put an end to its traditional indifference toward the Korean peninsula. The trusteeship plan envisioned by Roosevelt was an attempt, by U.S. initiative, to adjust the conflict of interests over Korea between China and the Soviet Union. It also reflected U.S. concern for its own strategic advantage as well as the future independence of Korea. It was designed to balance strategically the continental and the maritime value of the Korean peninsula by placing it under the joint administration of the major powers. However, the mutual distrust that grew between the U.S. and the Soviet Union after the conclusion of war with Germany made it difficult for the major powers to collaborate in the administration of postwar Korea. As a result, as long as the U.S. committed itself to the independence of Korea, the sphere-of-influence strife over the peninsula was destined to shift, in its major part, from a conflict between China and the Soviet Union to one between the U.S. and the Soviet Union.

Nevertheless, the U.S. commitment to the independence of Korea was not necessarily unconditional. Rather it might be called the beginning of a long conflict between "intervention" and "withdrawal." As already noted, the U.S. recognized little value in the Korean peninsula either in its global or in its Far East strategy because of Korea's dual-peripheral nature. Thus, its policy from the summer of 1947 till the outbreak of the Korean War was based on withdrawal from the peninsula. On the other hand, it may be said that the decisions to use the 38th parallel as the line of demarcation between U.S. and Soviet forces, to station

102. Charles Bolte testimony, June 17, 1949, U.S. House of Representatives, Committee on Foreign Affairs, *United States Policy in the Far East,* Part 2, (Washington, 1976), pp. 58, 95.

U.S. troops in south Korea for a long period, and to intervene in the Korean War, were based on a posteriori reasoning rather than prudent calculation. The decision to use the 38th parallel was a reflex action to prevent Korea from becoming "the Polish question transplanted to the Far East," while the decision to station U.S. troops in south Korea was an emergency response to the threat to the unified administration of Korea posed by the failure of the first Soviet-U.S. joint commission. As Ernest May has argued, the U.S. had two kinds of policies: calculated and axiomatic.[103]

Also, it is worth noting that these policies, like Roosevelt's plan of trusteeship, were the products of a peculiar combination of ideology and geopolitics. All U.S. interventions in Korea were deeply committed to Korea's independence and unification ideologically, while showing a concern for Korea's relation to the Asian continent strategically. This interpretation is supported by the following opinion, which was expressed by John Allison, the director of the Office of Northeast Asian Affairs, one week after the outbreak of the Korean War: "If we can . . . we should continue right on up to the Manchurian and Siberian border, and having done so, call for a U.N.-supervised election for all of Korea."[104] This opinion was further expanded to the view that a "free and strong Korea could provide an outlet for Manchuria's resources and could also provide non-communist contact with the people there and in North China."[105] With respect to the withdrawal from Korea, this meant virtual abandonment of its independence and unification, and indicated that the Asian offshore island chain was strategically the first line of defense for the U.S. in the Far East. Three days after the speech at the National Press Club, Dean Acheson, recognizing that south Korea would not be capable of defending itself against invasions that were either started by the Chinese Communists or powerfully supported by them or by the Soviet Union, gave the following testimony before the Senate Foreign Relations Committee: "Of course, if under the [U.N.] charter action were taken, we would take our part in that, but probably it would not be taken because they [the Russians] would veto it."[106]

It is essential to examine the geographical distance between U.S. and

103. See Ernest R. May, "The Nature of Foreign Policy: The Calculated versus Axiomatic," *Daedalus* (Fall 1962):661–662.
104. Memorandum by the Director of the Office of Northeast Asian Affairs (Allison) to the Assistant Secretary of State for Far Eastern Affairs (Rusk), July 1, 1950, *FR, 1950*, vol. 7 (Washington, 1976), p. 272.
105. Ibid., p. 570. In detail, see Barton J. Bernstein, "The Policy of Risk: Crossing the 38th Parallel and Marching to the Yalu," *Foreign Service Journal*, March 1977.
106. Dean Acheson testimony, January 13, 1950, U.S. Congress, Senate, Committee on Foreign Relations, *Reviews of the World Situation, 1949–1950* (Washington, 1974), p. 191.

Soviet policies as reflected by the closer political and military relations that were developing between the U.S. and Japan just before the Korean War, and by the militarization of north Korea between the fall of 1949 and the spring of 1950. It may be said as well that this was the geographical distance between the demarcation line urgently drawn at the end of the war against Japan and the containment line drawn on the basis of later strategic calculations.[107] The southward movement by the north Korean army was an aggressive action in the sense that it challenged the "prestige" of the U.S. and the U.N., and in the sense that it attempted to put political, social, and psychological pressure on Japan. However, on the other hand, this still remained defensive in origin in the sense that it was designed to counter the new U.S. strategy in the Far East. As already observed, this aspect of Soviet strategy in the Far East was consistent even in this period. Accordingly, the cause of the Korean War in the international sphere was similar to that of the Russo-Japanese War: there was a lack of mutual understanding concerning the duality of both strategies and Korea's strategic value.

### APPENDIX
The Duality of the Strategic Value of Korea

As illustrated in the Mongol invasions of Japan in 1274 and in 1281, in Japan's expeditions to Korea in 1592 and 1597, in Russia's southward movement during the Russo-Japanese War, and in Japanese aggression on the continent during the Meiji era, the Korean peninsula has historically played a role as a corridor when a land power thrust seaward, or when a sea power expanded onto the continent. Closely related to the geopolitical position of the Korean peninsula, the role it has played can be summarized as follows: (1) it provides access to the maritime province (Vladivostok) by way of the northeast flank of the peninsula, (2) it is contiguous to Manchuria along most of its northern border, (3) it faces Japan across the Korean Strait, and (4) it provides entrance to the Sea of Japan, the Pacific, and the Yellow Sea.

In this context, it is interesting to note that Edwin Pauley, who made an inspection tour of both north and south Korea as a special envoy of President Truman in June 1946, when the cold war was escalating, analyzed Soviet objectives in the Korean peninsula. In his analysis the strategic objects of a land power were discussed from the standpoint of a sea power:

107. See Yōnosuke Nagai, *Reisen no kigen* [The origins of the cold war] (Tokyo, 1978), pp. 24–25.

The possible Soviet objectives in Korea are as follows:

1. To provide Korea as a puppet state which would make possible a defense in depth in the event that the Soviet Union were attacked from the Southeast. I would anticipate the present Soviet thinking would be to deal with Korea as they did with Poland and Yugoslavia, namely, with a puppet government they will make a Sovietized trade treaty which will only exploit the Koreans.

2. To provide an encirclement, or one jaw of a pincer against North China and Manchuria (the industrial heart of a strong new China). The other jaw of the pincer would be Outer Mongolia (newly Sovietized) and Siberia.

3. To provide a similar encirclement or jaw of a pincer against Japan in the event that Japan were built up by some foreign power to use as a base against the U.S.S.R. The other jaw of the pincer would be the Vladivostok peninsula, Karafuto, and the Kurile Islands.

4. To secure favorable port concessions in the warm water ports of Ch'ongjin (Seishin) and Hungnam (Konan) and Wonsan, similar to the concessions in the ports of Port Arthur and Dairen.[1]

Note: If civil war continues in Manchuria, the U.S.S.R. might occupy Manchuria on the theory that they must protect their interest in the railroads and be able to communicate between Siberia, Port Arthur, and Dairen.

In other words, Pauley discussed the strategic value in the Korean peninsula in four dimensions: it could function as a buffer zone in the event of attack against the Soviet Union from the east; it could be used as a base for encircling Manchuria and North China; it could be used as an advanced base for operations against Japan; and warm water port concessions could be secured there. This suggests that the strategic value of the Korean peninsula was never composed of a single value, but is instead divided into two, that is, a maritime value related to Japan and the sea routes, and a continental value chiefly related to Manchuria, North China, or the Russian Far East. It is Korea's fate to have survived as a peninsular state connecting Japan and the strategic points in the northern part of the Asian continent.

An extremely crucial issue is raised as a result of two strategic values coexisting in the small Korean peninsula. In a conflict between one or a group of land powers and one or a group of sea powers, the strategic positions of both parties can be countervailed when each power aspires to one of the two values. However, the Korean peninsula suddenly emerges with extremely significant strategic value when either power tries to monopolize both values. Therefore, the present demilitarized zone not only divides the Korean people into north and south, it also serves as a demarcation between the land power, which attaches more importance to

1. Ambassador Edwin W. Pauley to President Truman, June 22, 1976, *FR, 1946,* vol. 8, p. 708.

the northern half, and the sea power in the southern half of the peninsula. Both the north Korean army's attack on the south in June 1950, and the U.S. forces' advance to the north exemplify the type of struggle that ensues when one power tries to monopolize both values.

It is of profound interest to discuss further the strategic meaning that the northern part of the Korean peninsula holds because this region has historically been not merely the scene of confrontation between sea and land powers, it has also played the role of a strategic point at the juncture of land powers. This is exemplified historically by the clash between China and Russia that began with the opening of Korea. Furthermore, it is worthwhile to note the function of north Korea in the present Sino-Soviet confrontation.

In conclusion, there exist two strategic values in the Korean peninsula resulting in two types of clashes between major powers; one between a land power and a sea power with the peninsula serving as a corridor, and the other between land powers alone over the strategic value of the northern peninsula. In the first case, the Korean peninsula would act as a buffer zone stretching from north to south, while in the second, north Korea would take the form of a strategic point along the Sino-Soviet border. Since the Sino-Soviet schism became evident in the 1960s, the Korean peninsula has been functioning simultaneously as a scene of confrontation between antagonists of both types. Despite a short interim due to the Sino-Soviet alliance, such a role has been evident since World War II.

# Upward Social Mobility of the Koreans in Hawaii

*Wayne Patterson*
SAINT NORBERT COLLEGE

## I

STUDIES of immigrant groups usually include an assessment of the group's relative rate of upward mobility and the speed and degree to which it shed the ways of the old world and adopted the values of the new. The success or lack of success in adjusting to a new home is frequently attributed to the conditions in the receiving country. But because this approach at best can provide only a partial explanation for the adjustment of an immigrant group to its new surroundings, researchers have attempted to refine their analyses by examining the values and traditions of the old country from which emigration took place. To be sure, the combination of old-country traditions and new-country conditions in the analysis of adjustments has helped explain the record of immigrant groups in their ascension of the socioeconomic ladder and their shedding of traditional values in the new country.[1]

Yet the addition of an analysis of old-country traditions and values to the explanatory model rests upon the assumption that the immigrants are representative of those traditions and values. That is, the analysis of old-country traditions in helping to explain upward social mobility in the new country is only as valid as the emigrants are typical. For instance, emigrants differ from their countrymen in at least one respect—their de-

---

1. Some representative works for East Asians are Betty Lee Sung, *The Chinese in America* (New York: Collier Books, 1967) and Harry H. L. Kitano, *Japanese Americans: The Evolution of a Subculture* (Englewood Cliffs, N.J.: Prentice-Hall, 1969).

sire to leave the homeland, if even for a short while. If the assumption of the typicality of an immigrant group cannot be justified, then the analysis of social mobility in the new country must be modified to take this divergence into consideration.

In addition to the need to question the assumption that the emigrants are typical there is a second assumption that needs to be questioned. This is the assumption that social mobility or adjustment in the new country is independent of events and conditions in the old country. Such a caveat is not as obvious as the first but will become apparent at length.

Broadly speaking, it is the thesis of this article that the adjustment of immigrant groups cannot be adequately explained solely by analyzing old-country traditions and new-country conditions. The model must include a close look at the immigrants themselves apart from the traditional order and also a close look at conditions and events in the old country.

## II

This essay represents a preliminary attempt to apply such an analysis to the Koreans in Hawaii. It is fair to consider Koreans in Hawaii as being practically synonymous with Koreans in America, for from the time of their immigration seventy-five years ago until recently there were about five times as many Koreans in Hawaii as in the entire American mainland. While the observations of this essay are limited to the Koreans in Hawaii, their import extends to include all of the Koreans in America.

Korea was the last of the three East Asian nations to have some of its population emigrate to Hawaii. About fifty thousand Chinese had come between 1850 and annexation in 1898. From 1885 until the Gentleman's Agreement in 1907–1908, about 180,000 Japanese arrived.[2] The Koreans numbered but 7,000 and came in the years 1903, 1904, and the first half of 1905.[3] All three of these East Asian peoples had been recruited for work in the sugarcane fields by the Hawaiian Sugar Planters' Association.

Since their arrival in America the more numerous Japanese have achieved middle class status, overcoming racial prejudice, discrimination, and the infamous relocation camps of World War II. Their almost phenomenal record of adjustment and upward social mobility has been

2. Romanzo Adams, *Interracial Marriage in Hawaii* (New York: Macmillan, 1937), pp. 31–32.
3. For the history of Korean immigration to Hawaii, see Wayne K. Patterson, "The Korean Frontier in America: Immigration to Hawaii, 1896–1910" (Ph.D. diss., University of Pennsylvania, 1977).

amply documented by scholars and has inspired book and article headings such as "Success Story, Japanese-American Style."[4]

While the Japanese-Americans have become the archetypal model ethnic group to be emulated by other, less-fortunate ethnic groups in America, little is known about the record of the Korean-Americans. This lack of knowledge is the result of the small number of Korean immigrants and the absence of substantial research. Preliminary findings indicate that the record of the Korean-Americans is definitely comparable to that of the Japanese-Americans. The following eight points illustrate their rapid adjustment and upward mobility:

- The diet, dress and habits of Korean immigrants changed quickly from Oriental to American.[5]
- Koreans left plantation work faster than any other ethnic group in the history of Hawaii.[6]
- Koreans recorded one of the highest rates of urbanization.[7]
- Koreans generally spoke better English than the Japanese or the Chinese.[8]
- Second-generation Korean children were staying in school longer than any other ethnic group, including Chinese, Japanese, and Caucasian.[9]
- Second-generation Koreans recorded one of the highest rates of professionalization.[10]
- Second-generation Koreans exhibited more liberal and egalitarian attitudes toward social issues than Chinese- or Japanese-Americans.[11]
- By the early 1970s, the Koreans had achieved the highest per capita income and the lowest unemployment rate of any ethnic group in Hawaii, including Caucasians.[12]

## III

It is clear that even though the Chinese and Japanese had a head start because of their earlier arrival, the Koreans adjusted to American

4. William Peterson in *New York Times Magazine,* January 9, 1966.

5. George Heber Jones, "The Koreans in Hawaii," *Korea Review,* 6, no. 11 (November 1906): 401–406.

6. Andrew W. Lind, *An Island Community: Ecological Succession in Hawaii* (Chicago: University of Chicago Press, 1938), p. 254.

7. Andrew W. Lind, *Hawaii's People,* 3d ed. (Honolulu: University Press of Hawaii, 1967), p. 50.

8. John E. Reineke, "Language and Dialect in Hawaii" (M.A. thesis. University of Hawaii, 1935), p. 202.

9. Thayne M. Livesay, *A Study of Public Education in Hawaii with Special Reference to the Pupil Population* (Honolulu: University of Hawaii Research Publication no. 7, 1932), pp. 71, 81.

10. Lind, *An Island Community,* p. 262.

11. Shin-pyo Kang, "The East Asian Culture and Its Transformation in the West: A Cognitive Approach to Changing World View Among East Asian Americans in Hawaii" (Ph.D. diss., University of Hawaii, 1973), passim.

12. *Honolulu Star-Bulletin,* September 10, 1973.

culture in Hawaii much more quickly. In general, historical accounts note the success of the Korean-Americans in one or more of the aforementioned items but do not attempt a causal explanation.[13] Sociological inquiries, on the other hand, have gone a bit further in attempting to explain the success of the Korean ethnic group. These studies, in noting the small size of the Korean group, argue that, unlike the more numerous Japanese, the Koreans were unable to maintain a separate existence either on the plantations or in the cities. As a result, the Koreans were forced to mingle frequently with other other ethnic groups.[14] This also helped to explain why the Koreans compiled one of the highest rates of social disorganization, including the highest rate of outmarriage, a high rate of mental illness, a high suicide rate, a high divorce rate, a high rate of juvenile delinquency and a disproportionate ratio of criminal convictions.[15]

These sociological explanations of the adjustment of Koreans are quite accurate, but they are based exclusively on new-country (Hawaii) conditions. Used by themselves, the limitations of these analyses become apparent when viewing other small groups that immigrated to Hawaii at about the same time, such as the Puerto Ricans. The Puerto Ricans exhibited similar rates of social disorganization but, unlike the Koreans, did not exhibit marked upward social mobility.

If these sociological analyses are supplemented by considering the

13. These works include: Kim Wŏn-yong, *Chaemi Hanin osimnyŏn sa* [Fifty-year history of Koreans in America] (Reedley, California: Charles Ho Kim, 1959); Warren Kim (Kim Wŏn-yong), *Koreans in America* (Seoul: Po Chin Chai Printing Company, 1971); Sŏ Kwang-un, *Miju Hanin Ch'ilsimnyŏn sa* [Seventy-year history of Korean-Americans] (Seoul: Haeoe Kyop'o Munje Yŏn'gu So, 1973); Yun Yŏ-jun, "Miju imin ch'ilsimnyŏn" [Seventy years of immigration to America], *Kyŏnghyang sinmun*, October 6–December 31, 1973 (28 installments); Lee Houchins and Chang-su Houchins, "The Korean Experience in America, 1903–1924," *Pacific Historical Review*, 43, no. 4 (November 1974); H. Brett Melendy, *Asians in America: Filipinos, Koreans, and East Indians* (Boston: Twayne Publishers, 1977), pp. 109–172.

14. The most prominent sociologists using this type of analysis are Romanzo Adams and Andrew W. Lind. Their causal model, linking small size with rapid acculturation (as well as social disorganization) can be found in Romanzo Adams, T. M. Livesay, and E. H. Van Winkle, *The Peoples of Hawaii: A Statistical Study* (Honolulu: Institute of Pacific Relations, 1925), p. 41, and Lind, *An Island Community*, pp. 252–265.

15. See Madorah D. Smith, "A Comparison of the Neurotic Tendencies of Students of Different Racial Ancestry in Hawaii," *Journal of Social Psychology*, 9, no. 4 (November 1938): 395–417; Bryant Wedge and Shizu Abe, "Racial Incidence of Mental Disease in Hawaii," *Hawaii Medical Journal*, 13, no. 5 (May/June 1949): 337–338; Richard Kalish, "Suicide: An Ethnic Comparison in Hawaii," *Bulletin of Suicidology* (December 1968); Andrew W. Lind, "Some Ecological Patterns of Community Disorganization in Honolulu," *American Journal of Sociology*, 36, no. 2 (September 1930): 206–220; Robert C. Schmitt, *Age, Race and Marital Failure in Hawaii* (Honolulu: Romanzo Adams Social Research Laboratory Report no. 34, 1962); Lind, *An Island Community*, p. 292; Adams et al., *The Peoples of Hawaii*, pp. 36, 38.

traditions and values of Korea, we might note that Korea, like China and Japan, was a society in which education was held in the highest esteem. This would certainly help to explain, for example, the high level of education attained by the Koreans in Hawaii. At the same time, we would also note that Korea was the least modern and perhaps the most conservative of the three East Asian nations, at which point we would be at a loss to explain why, for instance, the Koreans came to hold the most liberal views of the three East Asian groups in Hawaii.

## IV

Thus, even when taken together, a model consisting only of old-country traditions and new-country conditions is insufficient to explain adequately the adjustment made by the Koreans to Hawaiian-American society. It is at this juncture that we need to modify the old-country traditions part of the model and examine to what extent the immigrants differed from their countrymen. If the immigrants proved to be similar to the Korean population in general, we need go no further in this line of analysis. In fact, however, the Korean immigrants differed markedly from the majority of their countrymen in five categories: their religious, demographic, occupational, educational, and social background.

In a country where the traditional orthodoxy was based upon Buddhism and Confucianism, a majority of the Korean immigrants to Hawaii were connected in some way with Christianity. The promotion of immigration to Hawaii bore the stamp of American missionary support. Recruiting was carried out mainly by Korean Christian evangelizers in the cities, where there was relatively more American missionary influence than in the rural areas. Many of the immigrants had studied in mission schools, attended Christian services, lived in close proximity to American missionaries, or had friends or relatives with some connection to Christianity. The extent of this divergence from the traditional norm can be shown in that there were but 100,000 Christians in a nation of eight million. Missionaries were feared by the majority of the generally antiforeign population and there were still laws on the books limiting Christian activities. Thus the Korean immigrants, unlike the Japanese and Chinese immigrants, differed from their countrymen in religious beliefs.[16]

A second important difference between the immigrants and the majority of their countrymen was their urban residence. Fully half of the immigrants came from the Seoul-Inch'ŏn-Suwŏn area, and most of the remaining half came from the other large seaport cities scattered

16. Houchins and Houchins, p. 564, note the importance of church-related activities in Hawaii. See also, Patterson, p. 416.

throughout the peninsula. Such an urban concentration among the immigrants was not unexpected due to the location in the seaport cities of the branch offices of the company that conducted the recruiting. Yet at this time Korea was an overwhelmingly rural country. So in this respect also the urbanized Korean immigrants from all over the peninsula differed not only from their countrymen but also from the Chinese and Japanese immigrants who came from predominantly rural districts and from predominantly one section of their country.[17]

A third important difference was found in the occupations of the immigrants. As we might expect, based upon their urban residence, most of the Koreans, unlike the Japanese and Chinese immigrants, were not farmers. Their numbers, in addition to farmers, included common laborers or coolies, soldiers, minor governmental clerks, political refugees, students, policemen, miners, woodcutters, household servants, and Buddhist monks. Many were unemployed and adventurous young men. Unlike the vast majority of their countrymen, who were peasant farmers, the immigrants exhibited a hodgepodge of occupations within an urban framework.[18]

A fourth point of departure from the norm was the fact that the immigrants may have been relatively much better educated than their countrymen, with a literacy rate of about 40 percent. Not only were these immigrants perhaps much better educated than their own countrymen, they were also much better educated than their Chinese and Japanese counterparts.[19]

A fifth important difference between the immigrants and their countrymen was their nontraditional value system. For many of these young men, the city was not their birthplace. In the ten years prior to emigration, no fewer than three armed conflicts had taken place on Korean soil, uprooting many peasants and forcing them to the cities where, unemployed, they took up menial callings. Drought, famine, banditry, and oppressive taxes forced many others to abandon the countryside for the uncertainties of the city.[20] These rootless people, unable to perform the

17. Bernice Kim, "The Koreans in Hawaii" (M.A. thesis, University of Hawaii, 1937), pp. 85–86. See also, Katō Motoshirō, Japanese consul in Inch'ŏn, to Baron Komura Jutarō, Japanese foreign minister, March 29, 1905, Secret Document no. 6 (received April 8, 1905). "Kankoku seifu Hawai oyobi Mokushika yuki Kankoku imin kinshi ikken—tsuki hogo itaku kankoku no ken" [The matter of the prohibition of Korean emigration to Hawaii and Mexico by the Korean government—recommendation and protection]. 3-9-2-18. 1905. Gaimushō Gaikō Shiryō Kan (Diplomatic Records Office), Tokyo.
18. Bernice Kim, "The Koreans in Hawaii," pp. 85–86.
19. Warren Kim, *Koreans in America,* p. 11                          .
20. Bernice Kim, "The Koreans in Hawaii," p. 78.

required Confucian rituals at the ancestral graveyard and dispossessed of farms and perhaps relatives, became primary candidates for conversion to Christianity. For them, the prospect of emigrating was not frightening, and they were prepared to defy the Confucian dictum prohibiting emigration. Not only had they become accustomed to American influences and perhaps even Christianity in the cities, they had also become unable or unwilling to perform the required Confucian rituals. For reasons not entirely of their own making—wars, poverty, famine—these young refugees from the more traditional countryside had come to embrace the cosmopolitan, modern, and anti-traditional liberal influences that abounded in the cities and that centered on Christianity and Americans. Thus the point raised at the beginning of this article—that immigrants differed from their countrymen by being willing to violate Confucian principles through emigration—takes on added significance.

### V

We have thus far identified five factors in which the immigrants from Korea differed significantly from their countrymen as well as from the immigrants from China and Japan. We may now use these factors to assist us in explaining the upward social mobility of the Koreans in Hawaii.

It has been noted that the Korean children continued in school longer than Chinese, Japanese, and Caucasian children and recorded subsequently one of the highest rates of professionalization. While all three East Asian nations traditionally had a high regard for education, we may speculate that a possible reason for the superior record of the second-generation Koreans in school and in entering the professional ranks was the presence of a number of former students and lower level clerks among the first generation. Their presence may have given added impetus to the generational transfer of aspirations and ability—a quality that was not as prevalent among the Korean population at large nor among the Japanese and Chinese immigrants to Hawaii.

Other indicators in the rapid upward mobility of the Korean immigrants were their quick change in diet, dress, and habits from Korean to Hawaiian-American and their rapid acquisition of spoken English (or pidgin). This was in contrast to the Chinese and Japanese, who clung to their native dress, diet, habits, and language after immigrating. One observer wrote: "Koreans live well. They wear American clothing, eat American food and act as much like Americans as they can."[21] Another

---

21. Jones, "The Koreans in Hawaii."

report on the Koreans stated: "They buy American clothing and adopt American habits to some extent . . ."[22] Because of the necessity for the small Korean group to interact more frequently with other ethnic groups, it follows that the Koreans would be under more pressure to conform to the prevailing modes of dress, diet, habit, and language than would a larger group. The Japanese, on the other hand, could pass an entire day of working, shopping, reading the newspaper, or conversing with their neighbors using only the Japanese language, wearing Japanese clothes, buying Japanese goods, and meeting only Japanese people. Thus the rapid adjustment of the Korean group in these areas can be quite adequately explained by the sociological analysis of new-country conditions. Even so, we can use the social characteristics of the Korean immigrant group to refine this explanation. This added analysis suggests that this "Americanization" stemmed in small part from the fact that the Korean immigrants were mostly from cities where there was considerable foreign influence, most notably American missionaries. On the other hand, most of the Japanese immigrants came to Hawaii from rural southwestern Japan, where foreign influence was minimal. In language acquisition as well, probably very few of the Chinese or Japanese immigrants could speak English upon arrival in Hawaii. Among the Koreans, however, there was a small but significantly larger number who knew a little English, through either their training at mission schools or their association with Americans in the cities of Korea, giving the Koreans an advantage in acquiring English skills. As a corollary to this latter point, it should be noted that the small size of the Korean group meant that it was impossible to support Korean language schools for the second generation for more than a few years, while Chinese and Japanese language schools have continued to operate.

We have also indicated that the first-generation Korean immigrants left the plantations faster than any other ethnic group in the history of Hawaii and subsequently recorded one of the highest rates of urbanization there. There is nothing in the old-country traditions or the new-country conditions to explain these phenomena. On the contrary, Korea being overwhelmingly rural and abounding with peasant farmers, one would expect that the Korean immigrants would be accustomed to agricultural labor and be content to remain on the plantations. In fact, this was the very expectation of the planters when they began recruiting Koreans. The planter who went to Korea in 1902 to initiate the immigration wrote from Asia:

22. *Third Report of the Commissioner of Labor in Hawaii,* 1905. (Washington: Government Printing Office, 1906), p. 18.

I feel as confident as I can without positively knowing, that the Koreans will prove good laborers if we can get them to the islands. . . . They are lusty strong fellows and physically much the superior of the Jap. In rice culture and mining work they excel any other nationality and I can't for the life of me see how it is possible for them to prove other than good laborers for us.[23]

Yet the Koreans turned out to be only mediocre workers and soon left the plantations for the cities, where they turned to other lines of work. The planters had miscalculated in assuming that the immigrants would be typical of their countrymen, when in fact they were for the most part city people who were unused to farm labor. In this respect also the Korean immigrants differed from their Chinese and Japanese counterparts, who were mostly peasant farmers. Thus, their urban origins help to explain the rapid exodus of the Koreans from the plantations to the city as well as their mixed reviews as plantation workers. In terms of subsequent upward mobility, it should be mentioned here that simply by quitting plantation work, generally regarded as the lowest form of occupation, the Koreans by definition had already moved up one rung on the social ladder of success in Hawaii.

Finally, second-generation Koreans exhibited values and attitudes toward social issues that were markedly more liberal and egalitarian than those of second-generation Chinese and Japanese. Certainly such attitudes and values would not be predicted considering that Korea was perhaps the most traditional and conservative of the three East Asian countries. We might try to explain the acquisition of these liberal values by resorting to the sociological, new-country-conditions explanation of forced intermingling with other ethnic groups. However, this liberalism is better explained by reference to two attributes of the Koren immigrants themselves. First, unlike their countrymen and the immigrants from China and Japan, the urbanized Korean immigrants, even before their departure, had exhibited nontraditional, even iconoclastic, values by their adherence to Christianity and their rejection of Confucian propriety. Second, and perhaps more important, was the diversity, socially and geographically, of the Korean immigrants. Unlike the Japanese, who were a relatively homogeneous lot from southwestern Japan, the Koreans came from all over the Korean peninsula and from all walks of life. With differing accents, customs, and habits reflecting their diverse occupations and origins, their hallmark was their heterogeneity. This diversity made it difficult for an orthodox standard to be erected or maintained in Hawaii and may have promoted tolerance and liberal values which were subsequently transferred to the second generation.

23. E. Faxon Bishop to Charles M. Cooke, November 11, 1902. C. M. Cooke Papers. Hawaiian Mission Children's Society Library, Honolulu.

## VI

Up to this point we have looked at a number of indicators of rapid upward social mobility for the Koreans in Hawaii. Analyses of new-country conditions and old-country traditions and values have been found useful but limited in attempting to explain these indicators. For the explanatory model to become more rigorous it must include such factors as the characteristics of the immigrants themselves and the differences, if any, from those of their countrymen. We found that the Korean immigrants as a group not only differed significantly from their own countrymen in Korea but also differed from their Japanese and Chinese counterparts, and that it was precisely these differences that have helped partially to explain their different and more rapid upward social mobility.

In addition to the characteristics of the immigrants, there is a second set of factors that needs to be examined. This consists of conditions and events in the old country at the time of, and subsequent to, emigration. Such an analysis can add a psychological dimension to the analysis of immigrant characteristics already outlined.

Drought, famine, war, banditry, oppressive taxes, inflation, corruption, and the general malaise that accompanied dynastic decline characterized Korea at the turn of the century. One American missionary at the time wrote:

We have never known such unrest among the Koreans due to the excitement of so many going to [the] Hawaiian Islands to work on sugar plantations, and the dreadful hard times . . . . not that the crops here are so poor (there is a famine in other parts of Korea) but everything has gone up so in price and money is simply no good, which makes everything so uncertain. Still the Koreans go on building the palace here at Pyengyang in spite of the hardships, squandering so much money, and just squeezing the poor people to death. We can't blame them for wanting to go to America. . . . [24]

These conditions in Korea had powerful psychological consequences for the immigrants to Hawaii. Many of the immigrants from East Asia went to Hawaii intending to work hard for a few years, amass a goodly sum, and then return to their native land to live out their lives in leisure. They might also consider returning if they were disappointed in the life that Hawaii offered. The Japanese, for instance, had left a proud, nationalistic, and modernizing society. There was little, except perhaps boat passage, in the way of obstacles to prevent their return to Japan

24. Mrs. William L. "Sallie" Swallen to her sister, Jennie, October 9, 1903. Mrs. W. L. Swallen letters, 1901–1903. S. A. Moffet documents no. 6, 1890–1903, no. 176. Seoul.

after working on Hawaiian sugar plantations. This point can be illustrated by looking at comparative statistics. Of the seven thousand Koreans who went to Hawaii, one thousand, or one-seventh, returned to Korea. Of the 46,000 Chinese who went to Hawaii, about one-half returned to China. Of the 180,000 Japanese who went to Hawaii, 28,000 went on to California and 98,000, a little more than half, returned to Japan.[25]

The Koreans also had the option of returning and approximately one thousand did return to Korea. Yet the situation was different for Koreans. Simply put, they would think twice before deciding to return to the domestic chaos that characterized the last years of the Yi dynasty from which many had been refugees in the first place. Psychologically, unlike the Japanese immigrants, the option to return was not a practical one for many of the Korean immigrants. This meant that the Koreans were more likely to consider living in Hawaii as a long-term proposition, while the Japanese may have been more inclined to consider themselves transients or sojourners there. Such a psychological dimension was recognized by the planter who had gone to Korea to initiate the immigration: "I feel furthermore that as compared with the Japs they will be more permanent as they should have no home ties or at least should have none considering the way they are ground down at home, and the advantages they would enjoy in the Islands as compared with what they have at home should tend to make them a fixture."[26]

## VII

Another psychological aspect of upward social mobility must also take into account events that occurred in the old country subsequent to emigration. We have already noted that the Koreans went to Hawaii in 1903, 1904, and the first half of 1905, with three-year, nonbinding work agreements with the planters. While the Korean immigrants were laboring in the sugarcane fields of Hawaii, the independence of their homeland was snuffed out in November, 1905, when Japan made Korea its protectorate. Five years later, in 1910, Korea was annexed by Japan. As a result of these events many of the immigrants felt themselves stateless, stranded in Hawaii, and unwilling to return to a homeland controlled by Japan. Only a drastic change in the East Asian political situation could cause the Korean immigrants to return home. Until Korean independence (it would be forty years) they would have to "make it" in Hawaii.

25. Adams, *Interracial Marriage in Hawaii,* pp. 31–32.
26. E. Faxon Bishop to Charles M. Cooke, November 11, 1902. C. M. Cooke papers.

Thus Korea's domestic chaos and its extinction as a nation-state by Japan combined to force the Korean immigrants to become more closely wedded psychologically to a future in their new home of Hawaii than in Korea. A group of immigrants who for the most part regard themselves as permanent residents of the new country would be more likely to adjust rapidly and climb the ladder of social success more quickly than would a group of immigrants who regard themselves as transients. For the former, the future is in the new country; for the latter, the future is in their homeland.

## VIII

This article has attempted to explain the pattern of adjustment of the Koreans in Hawaii, and indeed in America. It has noted that the Koreans climbed the socioeconomic ladder more quickly than the Japanese, whose success has been highly publicized. In attempting to develop a model to explain this success story, we have shown that it is not enough simply to analyze the conditions in the receiving country and the values and traditions of the old country. A more complete model is necessary. The model developed here has suggested the addition of two factors.

The first consisted of an analysis of the characteristics of the immigrants themselves. Such an analysis showed that the Korean immigrants differed in important respects not only from the Japanese and Chinese immigrants to Hawaii but also from their own countrymen. Because of this latter finding, the analysis of the values and traditions of the old country needed to be modified to take this into account.

The second factor in a more complete explanatory model consisted of a psychological analysis based upon conditions and events in the old country prior to and subsequent to the immigration. The addition of this dimension showed that, unlike the Japanese immigrants, the Koreans regarded Hawaii as their home for the foreseeable future because of domestic chaos and Japanese imperialism.

A complete model to explain the rapid upward social mobility of the Koreans, or any immigrant group, must consist of these elements: an analysis of the conditions in the receiving country, the values and traditions of the old country, an analysis of the characteristics of the immigrants themselves, especially if they differ from the population at large in the old country, and a psychological analysis based upon conditions and events in the old country just prior to and subsequent to the immigration.

# The Effects of the Cultural Revolution on the Korean Minority in Yenpien

*Setsure Tsurushima*
KANSAI UNIVERSITY

### 1. Aims in Visiting Yenpien

Just before departing for China in 1976, nine professors and one assistant, the fourth delegation of the Japan-China Friendship Association, met to discuss what to see and where to go during their proposed trip to the People's Republic of China. At the meeting I suggested a visit to Yenpien, in the southeastern part of China's Northeast (formerly known as Manchuria), to see how the Cultural Revolution had affected an area where Koreans had traditionally been in the majority.

Yenpien is not very far from Ch'angch'un, which is enroute to Tach'ing, a place we were likely to visit. No objection was raised by the other members, but we were told by the Chinese Embassy in Tokyo that it might be difficult to visit Yenpien, and that we should check at the Institute of National Minorities during our stay in Peking.

Upon our arrival in Peking, an interpreter of the China-Japan Friendship Association asked us what and where we were particularly interested in visiting. The visit to Yenpien was mentioned as well as trips to Tach'ing and Shanghai. Later he returned to the hotel where we were staying to inform us that all our requests had been granted, and that we would visit Yenpien on our way back from Tach'ing. He added that we should refrain from calling the area "Chientao" or "Kantō" (Japanese), but refer to it instead as "Yenpien." "Kantō" was the Japanese imperialist term for the area, he explained.

I was delighted to hear that we would be allowed to see Yenpien, since, as far as I knew, we would be the first visitors from a noncommunist country to the area since the start of the Cultural Revolution, and the

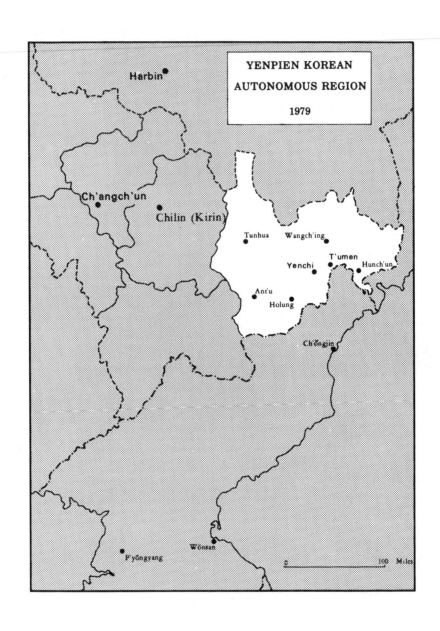

YENPIEN KOREAN
AUTONOMOUS REGION
1979

Harbin

Ch'angch'un

Chilin (Kirin)

Tunhua    Wangch'ing

Yenchi    T'umen
                  Hunch'un

An t'u
      Holung

Ch'ōngjin

P'yōngyang    Wōnsan

0                    100 Miles

second Japanese visitors since the 1949 Revolution. The last Japanese visit was made by Professor Hikotarō Andō in 1963.[1]

The Koreans in Yenpien are in a position similar in many respects to that occupied by any other minority in China. In assessing the situation of the minorities in China, it is important to note that while the Chinese government is anxious to emphasize that China is peopled by about fifty different nationalities, the Han Chinese comprise 94 percent of the population while other nationalities comprise only 6 percent. Although the right to independence is not granted, national minorities are given the right to autonomous government. Equality of all nationalities, as well as the protection of rights and identities of national minorities are policies that the government insists are important. But it is not easy to implement such policies when Han Chinese are in such a numerically dominant position.

To provide for self-determination by national minorities, autonomous areas have been established ranging from province, to region, to county, to people's commune. The following rank as autonomous provinces: Inner Mongolia (Mongols), Sinkiang (Uighurs), Ningsia (Chinese Moslems, referred to as Hui by the Chinese), Kwangsi (Chüang), and Tibet. In addition, there are twenty-nine autonomous regions, like Yenpien Korean Autonomous Region, and sixty-nine autonomous counties, like Changpai Korean Autonomous County. The extent to which any of these autonomous areas is allowed freedom of self-government depends on its geographical location.

Most national minorities live on the frontiers of China, and in many cases national borders divide them so that a group may actually live in two or more countries. Therefore, China's external relations with neighboring countries greatly influence the degree of self-government in such autonomous areas. The greater the tensions that exist between China and her neighbors, the more anxious the government is to maintain control over the border areas. All people living in border areas are, of course, expected to show loyalty and patriotism toward their country, but the need for unswerving loyalty particularly applies to national minorities living along the border. The government is aware of a potential for fraternization among minority members living on opposite sides of the border. It is also aware that if hostility to the government exists among national minorities, the affected border areas become more vulnerable, and the threat of invasion by a foreign power becomes greater. The need for de-

1. For the accounts of the area by Professor Andō, see his two articles: Andō Hikotarō, "Yenpien kikō" [Travels to Yenpien] *Tōyō Bunka,* no. 36 (June 1964):21–70; and "Kirinshō Yenpien chōsenzoku Jichishu" [The Yenpien Korean Autonomous Region in Kirin Province], *Chūgoku kenkyū geppō,* no. 193 (March 1964):1–29.

fensive deployment of many outsiders, especially army personnel, in minority areas makes mutual understanding between nationalities vital to national defense and makes the Han language an important communication link between people speaking different native tongues. Most Koreans living in China live along borders and are a case in point. Both Yenpien Korean Autonomous Region and Changpai Korean Autonomous County are located along China's border with Korea, and Yenpien shares a border with Russia as well.

From one standpoint then, unity of all nationalities throughout the country should be stressed, and conformity rather than diversity among nationalities should be the keynote, but these practical considerations tend to conflict with the ideal of autonomy for national minorities.

My particular interest in Yenpien Korean Autonomous Region was twofold. First, it was based on a broader interest in the effects of the Cultural Revolution on Chinese policies toward national minorities. Second, it was based on a desire to compare the status and attitudes of the Koreans in Yenpien with the Koreans in Japan.

During the Cultural Revolution, a great deal of propaganda was issued emphasizing possible aggression by "hegemonistic powers," particularly Russia, and defense along the border with Russia became a priority issue. During this period, the government may have felt the need to strengthen its grip on the area. It was of interest to me to try to gauge what effect the fear of possible Russian aggression has had on the degree of autonomy existing in Yenpien Korean Autonomous Region.

This information is of special interest in relation to the policies of other governments toward their Korean minorities. For instance, the Koreans who once had lived on the Siberian side of the border were forced to move to Central Asia in 1938 as a security measure.[2] As a consequence, very little direct contact exists anymore between Koreans living in China and Russia. The only chance they have to meet nowadays is if they happen to go to North Korea at the same time. Even on these occasions, however, meetings between different delegations of overseas Koreans are discouraged by their respective governments, and by that of North Korea as well. Once, when I was flying back from Pyongyang to Khabarovsk, for example, I saw two groups of Koreans, one from Japan, the other from Russia; they were sitting separately.

The only Koreans from other countries with whom the Yenpien Koreans can have contact are those living in North Korea, but even relations between Koreans in China and North Korea are far from good. The rea-

2. For the move from the Russian Maritime Province to Central Asia, see among others, Chong-sik Lee and Ki-wan Oh, "The Russian Faction in North Korea," *Asian Survey,* 8, 4 (April 1968):270–288.

son for this is that one of the features of the Cultural Revolution was the personality cult of Mao Tse-tung. When adulation of Chairman Mao was running high in China, adulation of the Great Leader Kim Il Sung was also gaining momentum in North Korea. Koreans in Yenpien naturally had to pledge their allegiance to one or the other and eventually settled on Mao, although there were reports of conflict over this issue.

The choice of Mao however, did not by any means settle the problem. Many Koreans in Yenpien have relatives and family members in North Korea who chose Kim Il Sung, creating conflicting familial and national loyalties that became strained as the fervor for the respective national symbols increased. The present delicate, triangular relations between China, the Soviet Union, and North Korea also serve to aggravate the situation. The more friendly North Korea becomes toward the Soviet Union, and the closer the relations between Yenpien Koreans and their families in North Korea tend to be, the more apprehensive the government becomes about maintaining control over Yenpien.

Another feature of the Cultural Revolution bearing directly on the minority problem was the "remember bitterness" campaign. It was designed to make the harsh conditions prior to the liberation stand out against the better life in new China. In Yenpien, however, such a campaign was a double-edged sword with potential for both integrating and alienating Koreans, because the struggle in this region involved the development of Korean nationalism as well as the overthrow of Japanese imperialism and landlord collaborators. It was in Yenpien that the Korean patriotic movement against the Japanese established its base even before the annexation of Korea by Japan. It was also in Yenpien that the most severe struggles for the independence of Korea occurred. In fact, Yenpien represents for North Korea a kind of sacred birthplace of the Korean Revolution. Yet all the significance of this aspect of Yenpien's history, which could serve as a stimulus for Korean nationalism, has not always been appreciated or welcomed in China. The choice of which historical lessons to learn is still a sensitive issue.

For instance, the Museum of the Revolution in Pyongyang exhibits many things related to Yenpien. However, the exhibits are exclusively connected in some way or other with Kim Il Sung, and items not related to him, but which had an important bearing on the struggle against Japanese rule, are deliberately omitted. Nevertheless, the danger exists that Korean nationalism among Yenpien Koreans, aroused by their forefathers' struggle in Yenpien, could lead to identification with North Korea and a feeling of kinship with those who idolize Kim Il Sung. It is unclear what the probability of such a trend is, but there is little doubt that the Peking government would oppose any such tendency, particularly at times when China's relations with North Korea are not good. The stories of Korean struggles in Yenpien prior to the liberation that are flattering to the Pyongyang govenment will not be well received in China as long as personality cults prevail in either country. Given these difficulties, how was the campaign to learn from the history of the preliberation struggle conducted in Yenpien, and what aspects of the struggle were Korean youth in the area instructed to study during the Cultural Revolution?

Yet a third feature of the Cultural Revolution was the *Hsiafang* movement, one aspect of which was the dispatch of youth to the frontiers. Numerous Han youth cadres went voluntarily or were ordered to the frontier areas where they often joined struggles against the local leadership. Although the Cultural Revolution fell short of its radical ideals, its successes included the removal from office of many entrenched powerholders, and the upgrading of the level of collectivization.

In Yenpien, one of those removed was Chu Te-hai, the first party secretary of the region, and the most prominent figure among Koreans in China.[3] Chu was the son of a poor Korean peasant in Siberia whose family was forced to move to Heilungkiang Province when the Japanese intervened in Siberia in 1918. After participating in an antiimperialist campaign, he was sent to Moscow University for education, and subsequently went to Yenchi, the main city in Yenpien, to rejoin the partisan fight in the Northeast. He spent some of the war period in Yenan, but returned to Yenchi at the time of its liberation after having participated in the civil war elsewhere in the Northeast. When the Cultural Revolution broke out, he was the only Korean alternate member of the Central Committee of the Communist party, and vice-governor of Kirin Province. The denunciation of a man with Chu's credentials could only have happened in the extraordinary atmosphere brought on by the Cultural Revolution.[4]

Chu was denounced in August 1968 as "China's Kruschchev representative, a nationalist factionalist, local nationalist, and would-be monarch of an independent kingdom." He was also charged with "obviously employing the theory of national social characteristics to cloak his activities." How he came to be denounced, and how many Koreans joined in his denunciation, is unknown. However, it is easy to see the lines of conflict between the local Korean leaders, talented in production and capable in many other respects, and the radical newcomers enthusiastically involved in politics.

3. For biographical information on Chu Te-hai, see Donald Klein and Ann B. Clark, *Biographical Dictionary of Chinese Communism* (Cambridge: Harvard University Press, 1971):1, 254–256.

4. Andō Hikotarō, "Yenpien kikō," *op. cit.*

In assessing the situation in Yenpien we must not overlook those aspects which differentiate it from other minority areas. Yenpien's Korean leaders have had a long association with the Communist movement, and Yenpien's high level of productivity and relatively high standard of living have led to a wide diffusion of education. By contrast, in other national minority areas, where people were backward in terms of productivity and living conditions, working teams sent as specialists on national minority problems could use the advantages of their advanced education and medical knowledge as leverage to coerce local minority people to move in the desired direction. In Yenpien, on the other hand, despite their knowledge of Communist party and government documents, young Han cadres found it impossible to force their views on local leaders. They found that established Korean leaders with long careers as Communists were well versed, and perhaps even better versed than they, in the theoretical literature.

Because of the ideological and generation gaps existing between the established Korean Communist leaders and the idealistic young newcomers, the two groups interpreted the situation in Yenpien in different ways. The different interpretations became exaggerated and grew out of all proportion due to the extreme conditions existing at the time of the Cultural Revolution. From the point of view of the leaders in Yenpien, it was essential that a high level of productivity and a relatively high standard of living be maintained or even raised. This they regarded as both necessary and important because North Korea, with a relatively high level of productivity for a third world nation, was always present as a comparison. Stagnation of productivity and a lower standard of living could easily cause demoralization of Koreans in their area. Such a situation could not be excused in their view, since it would invariably leave the populace open to the influence of the personality cult of Kim Il Sung. But from the point of view of the young Han cadres, endeavors to promote and maintain high levels of productivity and a relatively high standard of living meant that the leaders were "economists."[5] The terminology of the denunciation of Chu as a "nationalist factionalist, local nationalist, and would-be monarch of an independent kingdom" should be understood in this context. Thus the migration of large numbers of Han youth to the frontiers, and the influence they had on those areas, is in itself an interesting subject, but the impact they had on Yenpien deserves special study.

Since I am a Japanese involved in minority problems, my interest in

5. During the Cultural Revolution, the term "economism" meant the practice of using wage and other material incentives to undermine the revolutionary fervor of the people by luring them away from the Maoist line.

Yenpien extends beyond the events surrounding the Cultural Revolution. This is especially the case since the largest minority group in Japan is Korean. Moreover, although there were already 200,000 Koreans in Yenpien in 1910, most of the 1.5 million Koreans in China's Northeast at the end of the Second World War came after that date, just as almost all of the 2 million Koreans in Japan in 1945 came after 1920. Thus we can say that the Koreans in Yenpien and Japan left Korea at approximately the same time. The two populations are also roughly the same, with about 670,000 Koreans residing in Japan and about 730,000 in Yenpien.

However, the Koreans in Yenpien and the Koreans in Japan differ in one major characteristic. The Koreans in Yenpien consider themselves to be Chinese nationals, while, even after two or three generations, most of those in Japan are proud of being nationals of either the Republic of Korea or the Democratic People's Republic of Korea. Koreans in Japan face various kinds of discrimination. Because of this discrimination, second- or third-generation Koreans in Japan are very nationalistic regarding Korea, even though they speak Japanese as their native tongue, attend Japanese schools, and are almost entirely Japanized in lifestyle. On the other hand, it is in Yenpien in particular that Koreans should be filled with nationalistic pride, for it was there that Koreans united against the Japanese in their struggle for freedom and independence. Therefore, it was of interest to me to discover how the principle of equality among a multinational people materialized in China and how the present-day Koreans living in Yenpien view Korean nationalism. These were questions that could not be completely answered during such a short trip, but partial answers were suggested by some of the things we saw.

### 2. Outline of Yenpien

I woke up early, while it was still dawn; the change in scenery from the previous night was immediately noticeable. In other parts of the Northeast we had seen scarcely any mountains, only a vast plain. Broad, extensively cultivated fields had stretched in all directions. It was the season when water from the river, which lacked solid banks or dykes, seeped slowly into the fields, eventually flooding them. The first signs of Yenpien visible from the railway carriage were low hills surrounded by mountains. In contrast to the broad fields seen previously, every inch of the land in Yenpien was so intensively used for rice paddy farming that the large-framed, brown-coated cows, which clearly resembled the Korean species, were grazing in small groups along the river's banks, the only pasture available for them. Rice seedbeds, covered with vinyl frames to hasten growth and facilitate early planting, could also be seen.

The low-lying mountains around the valley were a mass of white pear blossoms; the scene reminded me of my visit to North Korea the previous year, where the land was also very intensively cultivated and where the hills also were skirted with orchards. Japanese descriptions of the area at the turn of the century say that Korean villages rarely had orchards, so I wondered where they originated.

Leaders of the Yenpien Korean Autonomous Region were waiting at the station to greet us, and after a hundred handshakes we were taken to the hotel designed for special guests. Yenchi seemed to be the only city in China where multistory apartments were being built at a great rate. In other places, people had seemed more concerned with the preservation of old houses. Again North Korea came to my mind; there too apartment construction is booming in the cities. There was similarity as well in the reddish color of the bricks used in the buildings. How had this similarity come about?

After a typical Korean-style breakfast, a youthful vice-president of the Revolutionary Committee, obviously from the People's Liberation Army, gave us an outline of the Yenpien Korean Autonomous Region. He explained that the Region lies on the frontier to the Northeast of Kirin Province, sharing borders with Russia to the east and with Korea to the south. The total area of the region is 73,700 square kilometers, of which 80 percent is covered with forest and 8.2 percent is cultivated land. The population is 1.7 million, of which 53 percent is Han Chinese, 43 percent is Korean. The remainder is made up of Mongolians, Hui, Manchu, and other peoples.

I was very surprised to find Han Chinese outnumbering Koreans, since in 1963 when Professor Andō visited Yenpien, Koreans still made up a little more than half of the population of the region. For the first time in the history of the area, Koreans were in the minority. I suspect this must be a direct result of the Cultural Revolution. Since the number of Koreans in the region in 1963 was reported as slightly more than 556,000, and since 43 percent of 1.7 million is 731,000, the Korean population had in fact increased. Therefore the change must have been due not to Korean out-migration, but to Han in-migration. I had known that a feature of the Cultural Revolution was the migration of Han youth to the frontiers, but I was surprised to find Han in greater numbers than Koreans. The purpose of the Han migration became clear when we examined the industrial development of the area.

Yenpien contains two cities, Yenchi and Tumen, and six counties.[6] Recently Tumen has developed from a small border town into a sizeable

6. The six counties within the Autonomous Region are Yenchi, Holung, Wanch'ing, An'tu, Hunch'un, and Tunhua.

city, with pulp and paper mills. The region, also has 111 people's communes containing 1,073 production brigades, and 5,225 production teams, and some towns.

Yenpien was officially liberated by the Chinese communists on August 15, 1948 (the third anniversary of the Japanese surrender ending World War II), and at that time a communist order was established. The liberation had come amidst struggles for land reform, which took place between 1945 and 1949. The land reform in the area was effective because of the previous history of the peasants' struggle against the landlords in the area, and because of the favorable political climate of the time.

In understanding the dynamics involving communist, nationalist, and class struggles, it is important to note that because Yenpien functioned as a base for anti-Japanese struggles in the twenties and thirties, a large number of Korean villages were beyond the reach of Japanese control. One must also note North Korean reports that land reforms and democratic legislation were first enacted in base areas near the Tumen River on the Chinese side of the border, a kind of rehearsal for the measures that were later used in the whole of North Korea. In Yenpien, therefore, the Korean peasants' challenge to Korean landlords not only aimed at improving relations between them, but also at distributing more land to the tillers. The persistent nature of the Korean struggle, supported by the bulk of the peasant masses, can best be understood if seen in relation to its inclination toward a class struggle, rather than purely as a nationalist movement. The first stage of land reform, which began in earnest around the end of the war, was quickly supplanted by another form of land reform, one which abolished the landlord system completely.

The occupation by the Soviet army after the war created a favorable political climate for the growth of land reform. Wherever the Soviet occupation took place, whether in Europe or Asia (including North Korea), the old order changed as people rose up against their former rulers and those who collaborated with them. But the special hatred of the Koreans for the landlord system and the latent desire for their own land was so strong that early struggles in both Yenpien and North Korea against Japanese and Korean landlords were quickly followed by total land reform.

In Soviet-occupied North Korea, the first stage of land reform officially started in October 1945. It was driven forward by the pressure of Korean peasants anxious to oust their landlords, particularly the Japanese and Korean collaborators who owned large amounts of land. It was followed in March the following year by a second-stage land reform, which took the form of a law designed to abolish the landlord-tenant system completely. Unfortunately, the processes leading to the establishment of land reform in Yenpien were not completely explained, nor was the relation between the land reform in Yenpien and that in North Korea, but the parallels are clearly visible.

While there are marked similarities in Yenpien and North Korea, the intensity which marked the struggle in Yenpien sets it apart from other minority areas in China. Early Chinese policies in other minority areas were based on compromise with local upper-class conservatives, and these policies survived even up to the Great Leap Forward and the Cultural Revolution. Regarding Yenpien, it is significant that the period of land reform, as cited by the vice-chairman of the Revolutionary Committee, was from 1945 to 1949, that is, between the year when Japan surrendered and the year when the Chinese Communist party took power. Thus land reform in Yenpien had already been successfully carried out when the new government came to power.

According to the local explanation, the establishment of the Autonomous Region brought significant changes to the area, and these have been further stimulated by the Cultural Revolution. Politically, people of different backgrounds have become the owners of the state, and equality among different nationals has become of special importance. The region, the people's communes, and the production brigades hold people's conferences to discuss and pass resolutions. Koreans have better representation at the people's conferences and are in more positions of leadership than their proportion of the population warrants. Despite the fact that the Koreans have become a minority group, 53 percent of the party leaders are Korean and 50 percent of the posts in the local government of the region and its counties are allocated to Koreans.

The Korean language is recognized as an official language alongside Mandarin Chinese. The official organ of the region, *Yenpien jih-pao* [Yenpien Daily], is published in both Korean and Chinese, and radio and television broadcasts are bilingual as well. Ninety percent of the villages under region administration have their own wire broadcast systems in Korean. All public notices are issued in both Korean and Chinese, while most private ones are in either one or the other.

In schools that are bilingual, both languages are used; but there are also Korean schools attended by Korean children who are taught Korean, and Han schools for Han children who are taught Mandarin. Generally speaking, most children pass through primary and middle school stages. However, there has been a movement to encourage more children from both Korean and Han families to attend ten-year binational schools, combining primary and middle school courses. At present the region has

1,379 primary schools and 210 middle schools. This is about double the number in 1959, when there were 505 and 141 respectively.

Koreans have traditionally placed great emphasis on education, and Koreans living in Yenpien are no exception. Even at the beginning of the century when Koreans were much poorer than the Han people in the area, Koreans had more schools. More schools were founded in Yenpien as a result of the "patriotic cultural enlightenment movement," a movement that reached its peak after 1905 and tried to stimulate Korean nationalism by concentrating on culture and enlightenment. One of them was Yi Sang-sŏl's Swiss school. Yi Sang-sŏl was himself the leader of the secret mission sent by the Korean emperor to the 1907 Peace Conference held at the Hague. He set out on that mission from Yenpien.

It was because of this traditional background that the Korean population was generally better educated than the Han. At the time of liberation, an estimated 84 percent of Koreans were literate. The establishment of a People's Government in Yenpien in August 1948 was quickly followed by the founding of Yenpien University. The early founding of the university was a natural development following the wide diffusion of education in the area; 1951 figures show that more than 90 percent of Korean children attended school, which gave rise to an interest in and a need for higher education. By 1959, Yenpien was known as China's leader in terms of literacy. Education was not only widely diffused but Yenpien students ranked highest academically of all the national minority areas.

The university consisted of three colleges—educational, medical, and agricultural. However, during the Great Leap Forward in 1958, the medical and agricultural colleges became independent. Today, besides the university and colleges, there are three technical schools in trade and finance, art, and education. The total number of students is 450,000, a quarter of the population, and 50 percent more than before the Cultural Revolution.

Local leaders like to emphasize the interest shown by the Communist party and the central government in the Koreans in the area by pointing out that the establishment of the university took place even before the liberation of China as a whole, and that such important visitors as Chou En-lai have made a special point of coming to see the area for themselves.

Yenpien is also especially fortunate to receive a budget for education which is three times higher than that allocated to Han areas. The higher budget is needed because many materials, such as textbooks, have to be published in two languages and bilingual facilities are expensive. But comparing the present situation with that which Professor Andō reported, Mandarin, as a result of the Cultural Revolution, has become an essential aid for communication. University and college courses now use only Mandarin and all the wall posters we saw were written in the same language. In 1963, however, professors were allowed to lecture in either language, and the preference tended toward Korean. At Yenpien University, Korean students are encouraged to select the Mandarin course so that they can become teachers of Mandarin, while Han students are encouraged to study Korean for the same reason.

A few years ago a conference was held under the auspices of the Central Committee of the Communist party to discuss matters related to publications for national minorities. As a result, the three northeastern provinces, Kirin, Heilungkiang and Liaoning, have an interprovince organization to promote publications for national minorities. The publisher for national minorities now publishes 350 kinds of books and booklets in Korean every year, twice as many as before the Cultural Revolution, so that ordinary Korean people can have access to important documents in their own language.

Accommodation of ethnic differences can be seen in the area of entertainment as well. There are three professional groups involved in entertainment in the region: a song and dance troupe, a traditional play troupe, and a Peking Opera troupe. There are also cultural song and dance troupes (seven Korean and one Han), and each production brigade has its own cultural and educational propaganda group. Each production team also has its own evening course for political discussion.

One of the notable achievements of the Cultural Revolution has been the extension of public health services throughout the countryside, made possible by the thousands of so-called barefoot doctors. The network of medical facilties is extensive, spreading from the main Yenpien Hospital through sanatoriums scattered throughout the region. There are more than 1,100 branch medical stations, and every people's commune has its own clinic. Likewise, production brigades have cooperative medical stations. The cooperative medical stations were begun around 1969, and in principle, are run by the members of the brigade. An adult pays a basic two yuan annually, a child one yuan, while patients receiving treatment pay a twentieth of a yuan for each treatment. There are midwives and nurses attached to the production teams, while doctors, assisted by nurses, man the clinics and cooperative medical stations. Both Oriental and Western forms of medicine are practiced, but many of the drugs are derived from natural sources, such as local herbs collected by people at the medical centers; and these tend to be preferred.

The backbone of the economy in Yenpien consists of agriculture and forestry. The most important crop is rice, which makes up a third of total crop production, (other crops being soybeans, millet, and corn). Rice production in Yenpien, carried out by Koreans, has an interesting history. At the turn of the century, millet and corn, not rice, were the staple foods of both Koreans and Chinese, while soybeans were the main cash crop.

Paddy cultivation was introduced about that time by Korean peasants, whose skill and toil enabled them to surmount many difficulties and make production feasible. The damp land, which Chinese farmers and peasants were loath to cultivate, had been allocated to Korean peasants, who applied their skill to convert it into paddy fields. By the 1920s, through gradual improvement of their techniques and the irrigation system and through the use of better seeds, paddy fields came to be more productive and to have a higher value than the dry fields. The expansion of paddy cultivation was not limited to Yenpien but also occurred in other parts of the Northeast as well, with Koreans being the chief cultivators. Paddy cultivation is still largely in the hands of the Koreans, although a few Han engineers work on the machines associated with such agriculture.

Agricultural yields have been increased by other means as well. Since the Cultural Revolution, great emphasis has been laid on increased mechanization in agriculture. There are now more than 1,000 large- or medium-sized tractors and 4,000 hand cultivators, compared with 150 and 50 machines respectively, before the Cultural Revolution. The tendency has been away from the larger Russian-style tractors and toward smaller machines, which are more versatile in small fields and are easier to handle. The move was not only for convenience's sake, but was also part of a conscious effort to give young Han engineers the opportunity to fit into the agricultural scene. Of course, Koreans are themselves every bit as capable of handling the mechanical side. The same tendency to introduce more but smaller machines can also be seen in North Korea.

In addition to soybeans and rice, tobacco and hemp should not be overlooked as major cash crops. Yenpien tobacco, which was originally cultivated mainly by Koreans, accounts for more than 80 percent of the tobacco production in the province. The area under tobacco cultivation in Yenpien covered about 115,000 hectares in 1959. The cigarettes we received enroute in Ch'angch'un were produced in Yenpien. Hemp, another important cash crop, has also been traditionally cultivated by Koreans, and the fibers are considered an important textile material.

The other mainstay of the economy is forestry. Much attention is paid to forestry because forests occupy 80 percent of the total area, and Yenpien contains a third of the whole forest area in Kirin Province. Kirin is second only to Heilungkiang in supplying China's timber. People are active in both forestation and logging; mountains are well forested, and evidence of the activity of the timber industry could be seen in the timber yards near the railway station, where piles of logs, usually aged twenty to thirty years, awaited distribution. The pulp and paper mills in Tumen are regarded as the most important in the whole of China. Because the timber supply is abundant there are many sawmills in Tumen, Tunhua, and other neighboring towns. The lumber industry has not only contributed to nearly every branch of manufacturing in Yenpien, it has also provided an important link between industries.

Apart from the forests, orchards, mainly of pear trees, extend onto even the fairly steep slopes of mountains. In addition, ginseng and other herbs that have been traditionally produced in the area, are now processed and packed in factories.

Although agriculture and forestry form the backbone of the economy in Yenpien, the development of industry, particularly in Yenchi and Tumen, has been remarkable. It is this development, apart from the troop fluctuations in the area, which has been the main cause of the population ratio shifting in favor of the Han. According to the official report, industrial and mining output has increased tenfold in Yenpien since the liberation, and since the Cultural Revolution, it has tripled. In Yenchi city itself, these figures are forty-five times more and four times more, respectively. The development of industry has been more rapid than that of agriculture, which has yielded a fivefold increase since 1949.

The main industries are iron and steel, textiles, shoemaking, machinery, and coal-mining. But in addition to these, construction of apartments, transportation of lumber, and printing, all of which we witnessed, should also have been included in the official description of the local industry.

In retrospect, it seems that the post-Cultural Revolution expansion of some industries, especially those closely linked traditionally with Yenpien and the Koreans of the area, may have been deliberately omitted from official explanations, but I am not sure why. Yenpien is particularly well known for the production of ginseng, antlers, and other kinds of Chinese medicine. These products, including ginseng, antlers, and bees' jelly, were readily available at the department store in Yenchi city, and we were told that production of these items had increased. Many people could be seen engaged in the production of veterinary medicines at a factory attached to Yenpien Agricultural College, and production there had also increased.

Silk production is also a feature of Yenpien, and the local people are justly proud of the improvements they have made in sericulture, for they have succeeded in breeding and rearing the silkworms for two cycles a year instead of the normal one. Wild silk is as widely used in Yenpien as it is in North Korea, and we were told that the quantity met the demand. But in the department store, where a lot of wild silk was on sale, some silk products were obviously made from a mixture of silk and synthetic fibers like those in North Korea, and it occurred to me that they might, in fact, have been North Korean imports.

In general it can be said that there is a wide range of industrial products available for the national minorities, and most of their daily necessities, such as rice bowls, pots, chopsticks, silk products, and knitted goods, are readily supplied. In this regard it was reported that commodity sales have increased sevenfold since the revolution.

### 3. Site Visits in Yenpien

#### A. THE PRINTING FACTORY

Our visits in Yenpien included a printing factory, a people's commune, a theater, Yenpien University, two colleges, and a department store. Our tour started at the Yenpien Printing Factory, where both Han and Korean workers were employed in printing materials in both languages. Banners of welcome and miscellaneous wall posters were written in both Korean and Mandarin. The factory was founded in June 1948, with an original work force of seventy using fifteen machines. During the Great Leap Forward in 1958, the factory expanded its workforce to three hundred workers, and began to print magazines. During the Cultural Revolution, it again expanded, branching into seven sections: type-picking, typesetting, binding, offset printing, machinery and graphics, and maintenance. The number of workers in thirty subsections had risen to six hundred and the capacity had doubled. They explained that mechanization and automation would be the next step.

Most of the workers in the factory were women, and the Korean workers wore Korean dress, probably because our visit was a special occasion for them. The apparently newer clothes worn by the younger women were thin, plain colored and devoid of pattern, in contrast to the older women who wore older, thicker, patterned material. Another point which drew my attention was that the older women, at least those over thirty, had permanently-waved hair and the style seemed to be uniquely Korean. Korean workers were engaged in printing Korean materials, for example textbooks for Korean study, while Han workers were printing science textbooks in Mandarin.

#### B. THE PEOPLE'S COMMUNE

We next visited Changpai People's Commune in the suburbs of Yen-chi city, the same one that Professor Andō had reported as being the most successful. The explanation about the commune was given by Mr. Pak, chief of the production brigade. He spoke in Korean; it was the first explanation we had heard given in Korean in China. The atmosphere of the audience completely changed as he spoke. Korean leaders who had listened rather passively to the explanations and addresses given in Mandarin at various other places, became increasingly relaxed and started commenting noisily about his speech. There was only one Han leader who could not understand Korean, and a Korean girl student staying at the commune acted as interpreter for him. It was obvious she failed to interpret everything, in spite of the leader's obvious interest in understanding what was said.

The people's commune, which became a binational commune in 1958, originated from mutual-aid teams founded at the time of the liberation. The latter expanded into primary agricultural cooperatives in 1952, and were reorganized into high-production cooperatives in 1956. The people's commune grew from these. The leadership of the production brigade is provided by a revolutionary committee composed of thirteen members (nine Koreans and four Han Chinese), with Mr. Pak as its chief. The production brigade consists of nine production teams containing 421 families and 2,145 persons (327 families and 1,620 persons are Koreans; 94 families and 525 persons are Han). Intermarriage is so rare between these two nationalities that so far there have been only three known cases.

Land under cultivation by the commune consists of 215 hectares of paddy fields, which Koreans cultivate; 102 hectares of dry land, which the Han cultivate; and 45 hectares of vegetable fields, which both nationalities cultivate separately. The brigade also owns some forest area and breeds pigs. A division of labor thus exists, with the Koreans raising rice in the paddy fields and the Han raising other grains on the dry land, although, as mentioned earlier, some Han youth work with machines used in paddy cultivation. The brigade owns eighteen tractors of various sizes, sixteen paddy planters, and a truck. Threshing and rice polishing is carried out using electrically powered machines. Eighty percent of the paddy planting is done by machine and the rest by hand.

Before 1949, 70 percent of the land that the brigade now owns was in the hands of landlords and was cultivated by tenants, while 30 percent was cultivated by owner-peasants themselves. Because of the high rate of rent, which was about 65 percent of the yield, incentive was low and the land produced only about 1 ton per hectare. At present the land reportedly produces 3 tons per hectare of rice, and 35 tons per hectare of vegetables. These estimates seemed to me extraordinarily high as the most favorable estimates in the West now put China's rice production at an er-

ratic average of 2.5–3.5 tons per hectare, and it is doubtful that production in Yenpien could exceed that of South China, even though it is
known to be the highest in the Northeast. Given the unfavorable climate
and growing conditions, it must be considered a prodigious achievement,
if the figures are anywhere near accurate, especially when compared to
the roughly 1.7 tons per hectare produced in the Philippines and 6 tons
per hectare in Japan—the former having near ideal climatic conditions
and the latter a highly developed cultivation technique. It is no wonder
that the leaders in Yenpien put special emphasis on this point.

The production unit is, in fact, neither the commune nor the brigade, but the production team. The harvest of each team is divided into
three parts: one for the government, commune, and brigade; the second
for members of the production team is divided according to the amount
of labor; and the third part is divided equally among member families. In
terms of percentages, 2–3 percent is paid to the government as a kind of
tax, 20 percent is set aside to cover the cost of further production, 13 percent is put into the team's reserves, 60 percent is paid to members of the
team, and less than 5 percent is divided equally among member families.
Of the 20 percent reserved to cover costs of further production, 2 percent
is put aside for various uses such as subsidizing medical facilities and so
on, while another 2 percent goes into the production fund.

The 60 percent distributed among members of the team is allotted
on the basis of a point system. Each process in the cultivation of the paddy is taken separately, and points are allotted according to the skill of a
worker in that particular process. The processes may be roughly divided
into ploughing, seeding, transplanting, weeding, harvesting and so on.
On the basis of his skills, a worker in any one process is classified into
one of several different skill levels. Thus a first-class transplanter gains
points because of the skill and hard work involved. A top-rate worker in
this category can gain a maximum of 20 points, while fewer points are
given on a sliding-scale to lower-rated workers, with 1.5 being the maximum number of points between skill levels. A worker in seeding, for example, is given a flat rate of 12 points and one who works on dry land 10
points. At the end of the season each member reports the total number of
points he has accumulated, and the team's share of the harvest is then
divided among the members according to percentages based on the total
number of points earned by all members. Each member thus has a rough
idea of how much he will be paid. Once it is established how much each
will receive, a meeting is called to discuss any necessary amendments.
After the adjustments, payments are made by the production team. The
average wage for a member is about 160 yuan per year.

Most of the plots of land for private production, which each family is theoretically free to cultivate, are in practice collectively cultivated paddy fields. The only really free private area for family cultivation is a small piece of land for vegetables. The brigade is self-sufficient in food. After paying taxes, it usually has accumulations of 750,000 yuan and 325 tons of rice reserves. At present the total savings of brigade members is about 20,000 yuan.

In terms of standard of living, the brigade has a wire-broadcast station, a library, and a cultural propaganda team with a film projector. Member families of the brigade own 832 clocks, 190 bicycles, 250 radio sets, and 230 sewing machines. Five barefoot doctors and ten nurses staff the brigade's cooperative medical station, and Mr. Pak proudly pointed out that there had been no cases of infant mortality since the Cultural Revolution.

Ninety-seven students from other parts of China were staying in the brigade community, living together in seven houses. Their living costs and labor costs for the first year were paid by the Central Government, but since then they have been paid the same as the members of the brigade. Twelve of them were members of the Communist party, and forty-four had received certificates of rural leadership.

After the explanation ended, we visited one of the houses in the brigade community. The owner, Mr. Kim, was about sixty years old and he was born in the same place in which he was living, while his wife came from a village about 15 kilometers away. Both greeted us in traditional Korean costumes. He explained that he receives about 4,600 kilograms of rice per year, of which a third can be saved. He reckoned that about 250 kilograms per capita is saved annually in the brigade. Mr. Kim's son was away from home studying at a cadre school in Kirin city. His daughter, who arrived while we were talking to him, was living at home with her parents and working on the land. She was dressed in working clothes commonly worn by young Han Chinese of her generation, and her hairstyle was also Han style.

Their house was a typical Korean peasant structure, built on a wooden frame with a thatched roof and mud walls. The one and only entrance was a door leading directly into the kitchen, which had an earth floor. A large brick and earth range provided not only facilities for cooking, but also heated the entire house in the Korean traditional manner by a network of pipes which conducted the smoke under the floors of the adjoining rooms. The smoke finally escaped through a large chimney on the other side of the house. The room off the kitchen (about 4 by 3 meters) acted as a combined living/guest room with a wooden floor covered by thin, woven straw mats. At one side, large storage jars containing pickles and other foods were lined up, and on the wall a single calendar was the only adornment. This calendar was interesting in that it showed a seated leader dressed in military uniform addressing a group of Korean peasants seated in a semicircle at his feet. The setting was a bamboo grove in the Yenpien area, and the leader bore a strong resemblance to Mao Tse-tung who, in fact, had never visited Yenpien.

The adjoining sleeping area, separated by a curtain, was divided into two and was the same size as the other room. One part was for the daughter and the other for the couple, although there was no special feature to indicate who slept where. The couple's side had Korean costumes hanging on the wall, as well as traditional leather hats, which gave rise to leg-pulling by the Han Chinese who were with us. Mr. Kim's wife became visibly angry. This kind of traditional Korean dwelling probably remains in any sizeable numbers only in Yenpien. In North and South Korea, they are being replaced rapidly by more modern structures.

### C. THE UNIVERSITY AND COLLEGES

Our third visit was to Yenpien University and the two colleges. As one might expect, they had been strongly influenced by the Cultural Revolution. Under the occupation of Maoist workers' propaganda groups, courses had been shortened, workers together with peasants and soldiers had priority of application, students were supposed to learn from them by living and working together, and the combination of theory and practice was held to be of the utmost importance. Teachers and students were expected to spend a lot of time at factories and at people's communes and on campus to apply their concentration to political discussions. Chiefs of revolutionary committees (at the time of our visit this was a title denoting those who were formerly called university or college presidents), were clearly, though not vocally, unhappy at the sacrifice of qualified study for the study of layman's level subjects.

It was revealing to witness the effort and endeavors made by students to increase production immediately by assisting in all the menial tasks performed by the peasants themselves, as well as their sympathetic approach to the peasants' revolutionary activities. Although such joint efforts undoubtedly have short-term benefits, the loss in terms of higher technical know-how may be felt in the long run.

*(i) Yenpien University.* Since the university's founding in 1949, the staff has increased from less than 50 to the present 464 and the student body from 460 to 1,400. As already mentioned, the medical and agricultural colleges became independent in 1958. Out of the 464 staff members, 60 percent were Korean, 40 percent Han, while the 1,400 students were a mixture of Korean, Han, Manchu, Mongolian, and Hui. The students were divided into seven faculties: politics, Chinese culture, Korean lan-

guage, mathematics, chemistry, physics, and athletics. Only the faculty of Chinese culture has three subsections, Chinese culture, Chinese language, and Korean language. The Korean language section is for the study of Korean literature, while the Korean language faculty is to teach the Korean language to Han students from all parts of China. Similarly the primary purpose of the Chinese language section of the Chinese culture faculty is to teach Chinese to Korean students.

The university has a branch in Wangch'ing with three courses: politics, physics, and athletics. Since 1970, only workers, peasants, and soldiers have been allowed to apply to the university. The courses were shortened from four years in the case of the athletics faculty, and five years at the others to three years. Subjects for students to study have been reduced from more than thirty to thirteen or fourteen. At the faculty of politics, students are expected to study the history of Western philosophy, the history of Chinese philosophy, economics (Marx's *Das Kapital*), the foundation of socialism (Stalin's works), and Mao's works on rural problems. Korean students of the Chinese language section were editing a Chinese-Korean dictionary by themselves, while Han students were preparing a textbook on Korean.

By maintaining solidarity with workers, peasants, and soldiers, students are expected to combine theory and practice by struggling for the three great revolutionary movements. These are the class struggle, the struggle for production, and the struggle for scientific experimentation. Students in the courses of social science or literature are encouraged to acknowledge real society as their classroom, while those in natural sciences are directed to try to solve practical problems in the struggle for production. By having contact with agricultural bases and factories, they are not only to retain a high level of political consciousness, but also to find and solve practical problems more efficiently. Students are expected to go to people's communes or factories as much as possible, even if this conflicts with classes on the campus. Teachers only spend a third of the four hours allotted to class time actually teaching; the students must use the rest of the time for discussion among themselves.

A chance arose for us to have a discussion with some students. Those attending included the chief of the revolutionary committee (Korean), the vice-chief of the Maoist workers propaganda team (Korean), two teachers—one of science (Korean) and one of Mandarin (Han), a Han student of the Korean language faculty, five Korean students (three males and two females) of the Chinese-language section, and a Han female graduate working at a people's commune. The students were shy and hesitated to speak.

In answer to the question of what they had actually learned in the people's communes, they explained that at the commune they had learned from Mr. Kim (the chief of the commune and a guest lecturer at the university) about education along the "general line" and how he had organized the brigade. The "general line" was a phrase originally coined by Mao Tse-tung to urge people to catch up with and surpass the United Kingdom in industrial production, to "build socialism by exerting the utmost efforts and pressing forward consistently to achieve greater, faster, better and more economic results." The Mr. Kim mentioned also happened to be one of the men whom Professor Andō reported as having been rewarded for the success of his commune.

It was of special interest to me to find that the students insisted that when they studied local history, they had to view it as a history related to other nationalities. But there was total silence when they were asked what they had learned about the heroic struggle by Koreans of the area against Japanese rule for the liberation of Korea and the Korean people. This came as a shock to me. After an embarrassing interval in which no one spoke, a Korean teacher, his face bright red, summoned up enough courage to offer an answer: "We are members of the Chinese people. The history which we should learn is Chinese history and local struggles should be studied in relation to the history of the Chinese Communist party. We teach Korean independence as part of the history of that country."

*(ii) Yenpien Medical College.* The college gained independence from Yenpien University during the Great Leap Forward. Scattered over an area of 12,000 square meters, it has 19 laboratories, a hospital with 500 beds, and a branch school in the countryside. There are about 300 staff members of whom 90 are teachers. They teach 600 students courses in medical science, pharmacy, and nursing. Out of about 3,000 graduates over the past twenty-four years, 1,390 have graduated since the Cultural Revolution. Since 1970, and at the time of our visit, only workers, peasants, and soldiers have been permitted to apply for entrance. Also around 1970 the aims of the college were reformulated so that students were encouraged to work together actively with workers and peasants in the countryside. The course was shortened from five years to two, and a new one-year course was opened in connection with a program for the people's commune.

Emphasis was placed on: (1) the improvement of thought, (2) the combination of fundamental theory and practice, and (3) the combination of thought and practice. Students were required to train not only at the hospital attached to the college but also at the county sanatorium and similar facilities. They were also expected to join together in groups and extend medical services in the countryside by living and working with peasants. Oriental as well as Western medical science was taught, and attention has focused on more common diseases. The Chief of the revolutionary committee sounded far from happy when he described the emphasis on common diseases like stomachache, diarrhea, colds, and appendicitis. As an attempt to maintain standards, he insisted that the students learn to manage a stomach operation by the end of the course. His feelings were understandable.

When Yenpien University, complete with colleges of education, medical science, and agronomy, was founded in April 1949, it fostered a revolutionary tradition, a wide diffusion and high level of education, and the advanced productivity of Koreans in the area. The only comparable institute founded around the same time by either the Communist party or the new Peking government was a cadre school opened on the frontier in Inner Mongolia in 1950. Yenpien was not the only minority area led by local national leaders in the age of communist movements, but the general educational level of the populace and high level of productivity have put it well ahead of other minority areas and even ahead of neighboring Han areas. Koreans in Yenpien were rightfully proud of the levels reached in medical science and agronomy at Yenpien University, but purely academic studies of a high level had been reduced to the common norm by the Cultural Revolution. The chief of the revolutionary committee at Yenpien Medical College must have found it hard to hide his frustration at not being able to show us something of their real academic intentions.

*(iii) Yenpien Agricultural College.* At the time of our visit, the college had 460 regular students in three faculties: agronomy, animal husbandry and veterinary science, and agricultural machinery. The faculty of agricultural machinery was subdivided into two sections, agricultural machinery and orchard management. In addition to this, there were over 10,000 students taking correspondence courses. The staff members and their assistants numbered about 70 leaders and 100 workers, who worked on mixed farms, on stock farms, in a factory producing agricultural and veterinary medicines, and in an implement repair factory. The course for regular students had been shortened to two years, and its aim was to produce leaders for production brigades or production teams.

Four hundred twenty students had graduated from regular courses since 1970, while those who attended shortened courses since the Cultural Revolution numbered about 5,000, of whom 60 percent were Korean and 40 percent Han. Thirty to 40 percent were women. Education was very much integrated into the work of the people's commune, and it was an impressive sight to see a large number of people busily working at the factory that was attached to the college and that produced agricultural and veterinary medicines.

Wedged between our hectic schedule of visits there were some lighter moments when we could relax and simply enjoy the warmth of our hosts' hospitality. Included in such moments were a trip to a theater, a department store visit, and some parties given in our honor. At a performance given by students of the special school of arts at a theater in Yenchi, we heard and saw traditional and revolutionary folk songs and dances, and other songs and dances that were a mixture of both. These were designed to stimulate revolutionary consciousness and a spirit of brotherhood among the different nationalities. I was quite surprised to hear a familiar song, which I had heard sung in praise of Marshal Kim Il Sung both in Pyongyang and in Japan, being sung for Mao Tse-tung instead.

The department store was crammed full of commodities and shoppers, more so in proportion to floor space than stores in Peking or Shanghai. This was probably due to both the rapid increase in the population and the failure of the facilities to keep pace with it.

I attended a party in Yenpien with students staying at the people's commune. We joined in the traditional Korean folk dances after a typical Korean meal, which was accompanied by large quantities of locally produced spirits. Old Kim, whose house we had visited, was also there and while dancing he said to us in Korean, "Long live Korean-Japanese friendship," which a Korean hastily interpreted as, "for the friendship of both peoples." The Han interpreters commented that he had obviously been a landlord before the liberation.

At another party organized by the revolutionary committee of Yenpien and other organizations, I asked one of the local leaders if Koreans in Yenpien were able to visit their relatives in North Korea. He replied that, thanks to an agreement concluded by Chou En-lai with North Korea, a Korean could now go to North Korea once a year if he wanted, but he neither volunteered any further information nor voiced any enthusiasm about the closer relations with North Korea. When I ventured to say that the journey to North Korea was simply a matter of boarding a train in Yenchi, which was based on information I recalled from the war years, he corrected me by saying that no trains could travel directly to North Korea because it was impossible to cross the Tumen River, and that passengers wishing to go there had to disembark, cross by boat, and reboard another train on the other side of the border.

### 4. Some Comparisons and Observations

On our return to Peking from Yenpien, we had the opportunity to meet Vice-premier Chi Ting-kuei and leaders of the Japan-China Friendship Association in the Great Hall of the People. In reply to his questions about why we had been particularly interested in visiting Yenpien and what our impressions had been, I pointed out the significance of Chinese policy toward their Korean minority as compared to that of the Russians or Japanese toward their own Korean minorities. Since in all three cases the Koreans had migrated at approximately the same time, each country's treatment of its Korean minority serves as a barometer of its inclination toward democracy and an unbiased minority policy.

The very existence of Yenpien Korean Autonomous Region along the border with Russia is proof that the Chinese have a more lenient attitude toward the Koreans than the Russians. This was not the case when Koreans first started migrating to Yenpien and Siberia. Russian authorities welcomed early Korean immigrants, and even tried to lure them to Siberia by the promise of grants of land upon naturalization, because the Koreans were needed to produce the fresh food necessary to support Russia's policy of eastern expansion. Similarly, early immigrants to Yenpien did not have to pay taxes because the area was officially designated as "closed," or prohibited to new immigrants. Later, after the official prohibition on immigration was lifted, immigrants to Yenpien had to cope with deteriorating political conditions. However, these conditions were overcome by the Koreans' skill in cultivating paddy and by their sheer hard work. Thus, although official Chinese and Russian policies differed, both areas received large numbers of immigrants during this period.

These early immigrants also had quite a bit of social contact with each other. Many seasonal workers, having worked in Siberia during the summer, wintered in Yenpien rather than returning to Korea. The migrants preferred to pass the winter in Yenpien because living costs were lower in Yenpien than in Siberia or Korea. The Yenpien Koreans welcomed them because they were good customers. For this reason, the Koreans in Yenpien were all the more aware of the fate of their brothers when the Koreans on the Russian side of the border were forced to abandon their land and move to central Asia in 1938. The Yenpien Koreans have not lost sight of the fact that they still cultivate land tilled by their forefathers, and that they now have a certain measure of autonomy.

Western critics have been all too ready to show up the limitations of autonomy which national minorities in China enjoy, pointing out that neither independence nor secession are permitted. Nevertheless, in comparing the conditions of Koreans in China and Japan, we cannot say that those in Japan are necessarily better off. Their situations differ on a number of points. Koreans in Yenpien work mostly on the land, while those in Japan are mainly engaged in industry. Since the productivity of rice is higher than other grains grown in the Northeast, and since Koreans are dominant in this type of agriculture, they are in an advantageous position. By contrast, Korean workers in Japan suffer from various types of job discrimination when seeking employment at major companies, banks, and most governmental agencies.

The contrast of situations extends to language policy as well. Korean is recognized as an official language in Yenpien and Korean children attend Korean schools to learn their own language. The government supports bilingual education by extending extra funds for this purpose. In Japan, on the other hand, government policy aims at integration by "Japanization," forcing Korean children to go to Japanese schools, although only Japanese children at these schools receive subsidized textbooks and lunches. The Korean lifestyle and national costume are protected in the same way as education in Yenpien, and the government ensures, through factory subsidies, that commodities necessary for maintenance of such a lifestyle are produced. Koreans in Japan are advised to change their Korean names to common Japanese names so that the procedure for naturalization can be smoothed.

One can argue that Koreans in Japan are free to criticize Japanese policies and to express their support for Kim Il Sung, Park Chung Hee, Kim Dae Jung, or whomever they like, while it is difficult for Koreans in China "to criticize the Peking government openly," to express their admiration of Park Chung Hee or even Kim Il Sung. However, closer inspection reveals that the politically free stance which Koreans in Japan appear to have in fact has severe limitations, since the immigration law prohibits any activity which Japanese authorities deem "political." The penalty for violators of this law may be loss of the right to live in Japan and deportation to Korea, a country they have never seen and whose language they cannot understand. This includes second- or third-generation Koreans, unless they have secured Japanese nationality. If forced to choose between a place where human rights are ignored or a place where autonomy lacks a clause providing for independence or secession, it is not hard to decide in which place the Korean minority is treated better.

We also saw in Yenpien how, in various respects, the lives of the people had been affected by the Cultural Revolution, but we did not mention the subject in the Great Hall of the People because time was too short and because of the sensitivity of the subject (it was just prior to the fall of the Gang of Four). In some institutions, like the university and colleges in Yenpien, we were told that they were promoting the integration of education with productive labor, and that they regarded Chaoyang Agricultural College as their ideal. Since the fall of the Gang of Four, the Chaoyang model has been dismissed as an "abortion," but during our visit we observed that students were spending more time at people's communes or in factories than on campus, and more time in discussions among themselves rather than attending classes or engaging in research. At other academic institutions like Peking University, however, the importance of theoretical study in science was admitted, and a prominent professor there even hinted at the necessity of enrollment procedures that included entrance examinations. During the Cultural Revolution, the policy was to send middle school graduates to rural areas, the armed forces, or industry for several years so that their political character could be assessed before they were nominated for a university. It was virtually impossible to enter a university directly from school by taking an entrance examination.

We observed a wide difference of opinion between administrators at Peking University and those at Yenpien University concerning what students should learn from their factory or commune experience. When students of Yenpien University were asked what they had learned at the people's commune, they vaguely referred to the class struggle. On the other hand, students of Peking University explained that their study at the'factory had something valuable to offer in the way of experience. If, for example, they found some bottleneck in the production process, they would attempt to solve the problem theoretically, so the practical aspects could then be dealt with by the factory managers.

It was not a surprise to find that Yenpien University and the colleges there were still firmly entrenched in the beliefs of the Cultural Revolution, as indeed was Chinghua University in Peking, although Peking University itself was trying to escape from such dogmatism. It was difficult to determine during our short stay whether the pride in academic achievement that the Korens had held at the foundation of Yenpien University still remained, or whether it had been swallowed up in the anti-academic turmoil accompanying the Cultural Revolution. Due to the difficulty of recruiting qualified scholars in Yenpien as compared to Peking or Shanghai, and because of the underlying ethnic situation which aggravates the problem, it appears that lasting damage to academic studies may have resulted. It is easy to sympathize with the anger expressed by the chief of the revolutionary committee of Yenpien Medical College. Not only had the Maoist propaganda teams disrupted college life, though only temporarily, but the abnormal situation they had created was certain to damage the quality of medical science in the long term.

One of the most noticeable effects of the Cultural Revolution in Yenpien was the replacement of the older established leaders, who had experience in administration and party leadership in the region and who had played such a major role in the liberation struggle, by youthful, inexperienced newcomers. It was also noticeable that, in spite of their elevated position in the region, the newcomers did not seem to command much respect from the rank-and-file leaders. This was evident when we visited the Yenpien printing factory and the people's commune. Although in general during our stay in China it was rare for us to witness a case where lower-ranking leaders failed to pay respect to those above them, and common for leaders, including those elevated during the Cultural Revolution, to maintain a sense of their position, the representatives at the printing factory and people's commune in Yenpien almost completely ignored the high-ranking regional leaders who were accompanying us, only greeting those who appeared to be friends of theirs.

Certainly democratization has been one of the most tangible results of the Cultural Revoltion, even if it has come at the sacrifice of experienced leadership and a certain dignity of office. At the same time, I wonder to what extent this hampers the leaders in their efforts to protect the interests of the people and to promote the special interests of the region. Not only did the leaders at the printing factory and commune fail to acknowledge the regional leaders, but there was also an absence of any eulogy for Chairman Mao. At most, they showed loyalty to the Communist party, although not with any marked enthusiasm, and other political subjects, such as unity or equality of nationalities, were bypassed in favor of their all-absorbing interest in production.

Another outstanding omission was their neglect of the topic of self-reliance, a subject that workers in Tach'ing, a major oil-producing area northwest of Yenpien, had been proud to talk about. Tach'ing has been regarded as a model for industry, not only because of the efforts and spirit of its workers in overcoming many natural obstacles, but also because of the emphasis the workers and their families place on self-reliance. We saw examples of this at a sewing factory where clothes were made from old remnants, and at the communal field, where families cultivated their own crops. Their pride was tangible, for varieties of home-produced soybean curd and kaoliang spirits were pressed on us at lunch. At an automobile factory in Ch'angch'un, we were told that workers and their families cultivated their own plots, either in a field owned by the factory or at a local people's commune. But workers at the Yenpien printing factory did not seem to cultivate any land, or at least they showed no pride in trying to be self-reliant. At the people's commune too, the information lectures did not mention anything about people working outside their primary jobs. In contrast, workers at the people's commune in Shanghai were encouraged to visit factories producing motor coils or light bulbs, and these visits were regarded as highlights in their experience. The women at the commune in Shanghai expressed a feeling of solidarity with the women working in the factories, which promoted a feeling of their own emancipation. At the Changpai People's Commune in Yenpien, no mention was made of emancipation, nor did we visit any factory of this kind; instead we were taken to a peasant's house, and attended a party at the residence of students from other parts of China.

In most of the places around Yenpien where we had the opportunity to talk to local people, it was clear that they sensed the impending shift in the political line, and they were reluctant to voice an opinion about politics. Instead, they seemed eager to express their interest in increasing production or to tell how life had improved since the 1949 Revolution.

It was curious how leaders of the printing factory avoided or chose to ignore political issues and other matters that had been deliberately raised during the Cultural Revolution, and which students from the same area were still debating. Naturally, we were not told why the two groups had such differing ideas, but one can guess at some of the reasons.

One natural conclusion might be the desire to keep the commune workers' minds on their work, that is, on increasing production, and off the unpleasant aspects of the sudden population increase caused by the influx of Han youth. Apart from their role in the power struggle, their very presence and the fact that they had to be sustained by the local economy would naturally lead to resentment by the local peasants. The campaign emphasizing self-reliance had the unwanted effect of encouraging peasants to look out for their own interests, including wanting the food they produced for themselves. But the presence of Han youth meant more mouths to feed at a time when other areas were not willing or not able to supply the increased demand in the Northeast. The people's concern over the increased demand for food was clear. When we visited Mr. Kim's house, he mentioned that when there were surplus vegetables, they were sold to the cooperative shop in the people's commune. This was interesting, since we had earlier been told that people were only allowed to grow vegetables for their own consumption and so should not have had any surplus. The purpose of this was to integrate the private plots of land, which amounted to 5 percent of the cultivated area, and which each family was theoretically free to cultivate, with other land belonging to the production team.

The only way to meet the increasing demand for food was to expand the area of paddy agriculture. But the expansion of paddy fields was, as always, limited by the irrigation network, a serious hindrance to any plan for rapid increase in productivity. Another problem was social. Since there was a de facto division of labor between the Koreans who cultivate the paddy fields and the Han peasants who work the dry land, any change of dry land into paddy would widen the difference in productivity between the Koreans and the Han. Even assuming that Han peasants could reclaim more land than they lost to paddy agriculture, the greater efficiency of paddy agriculture would cause the gap to widen. At the time of our visit, the Korean peasants were being requested to step up rice production, and Mr. Pak had no time for any of the slack season jobs that other commune members took up when the fields were fallow.

Perhaps another reason members of the commune were cool toward the more recent migrants was that many of the Han in-migrants in Yenpien were not connected to the commune, but were instead logging in the forests, working in the mines, and contributing toward the rapid population increase in the towns. Factory workers in the towns seldom tried to find work in the countryside, and were not needed there except in busy seasons such as harvest time. Even then, students and soldiers were more easily mobilized. The students were anxious to learn from the peasants, while People's Liberation Army soldiers could assist in many ways that the factory workers could not.

The influence of North Korea may be another reason the leaders of the printing factory and the people's commune seemed more anxious to emphasize the importance of production rather than other goals. This leads one to speculate about the extent of contact between Koreans in both countries. Many of the things we were told while in Yenpien seemed expressly designed to show up the difference between the Koreans in Yenpien and the Koreans in North Korea, and to emphasize their differing nationality. A typical example was the case of students at Yenpien University, who seemed to regard the history of Korea and Korean literature as that relating to a foreign country, while the Korean struggles against the Japanese in Yenpien were viewed in the context of the history of the Chinese Communist party. The only Korean literature they seemed to regard as their own was that written in Yenpien. Where was their national pride, which during the Korean War had raised their enthusiasm to such a pitch that many Yenpien Koreans had actively supported the North Koreans and fought alongside them? If the facts we were told are true, we must conclude that the establishment of two socialist countries on either side of the Tumen and Yalu rivers has served to sever former contacts and to hasten the integration of Koreans into the respective communities of each country. The implication of the remark that the train from Yenchi no longer passes into Korea is very clear.

Many questions related to ethnic ties were left unanswered by our hosts. Not one of the leaders volunteered to tell us if he had been to North Korea, and, in answer to the question of whether they had family or relatives there, one of them replied quite forcefully that he had none. Also, the number of Yenpien Koreans visiting North Korea each year was never revealed. Yet, there were indications that fairly close contact remained. Apart from the early influences, such as the species of cattle and other things brought in with the first immigrants, there were other post-Korean War influences, such as multistory apartments and the location of the orchards. The latter were clearly postwar influences because they did not exist in North Korea before 1950.

To the extent that this contact remains alive, economic and technological developments as well as improvements in living standards, all of which are quite visible in North Korea, quite likely act as a stimulus to improvement by providing goals for which to aim. If trade does exist between the two countries, dried cod from North Korea in exchange for soybeans from Yenpien, for example, then the introduction of technology would be the next logical step. Leaders of various ranks in Yenpien are undoubtedly concerned with higher productivity to enable Koreans in Yenpien to enjoy a standard of living similar to that enjoyed in North Korea. Similarly, the impact of South Korean development on North Korea affects Yenpien indirectly as well. As a result of this situation, Yenpien holds a unique position among the frontier areas of China in that it is more susceptible to international economic influences than most other places.

Another change resulting from the Cultural Revolution which drew our attention was the increasing use of Mandarin. At the university and colleges, all the lectures, with the exception of the Korean-language class, were given in Mandarin, and all the wall posters were written in the same language. Most of the speeches, including those given by Korean leaders, were in Mandarin. Certainly the use of Mandarin is necessary since so many in-migrants have moved to Yenpien. Mandarin has been adopted as the main language not only for the purpose of communication, but also to provide a common unifying base to ensure the peaceful coexistence of different nationalities. If, after the Cultural Revolution, emphasis is again put on minority identities, as was done in the aftermath of the Great Leap Forward, then the Korean language is likely to see a revival. But it is inevitable that in the long run such swings in policies will eventually lead to Mandarin gaining ground. The same thing can be said for the traditional Korean costume and hairstyle. Although we saw Mr. Kim attired in traditional costume at home, and women at the printing factory similarly dressed, it was obvious that they had dressed specially for our benefit. Usually they would have worn ordinary work clothes like other Han workers. Miss Kim was a more typical example of her age group, both in hairstyle and dress.

Although the Cultural Revolution certainly played a role in helping to narrow the differences between Koreans and the Han majority, it was impossible for us to gauge accurately how strong an effect it had. Many conflicting reports have been written. I have attempted through my own observations to analyze what the changes have been, and to show how Yenpien, with its unique geographical, historical, and cultural background, has been affected. At the time of my visit it appeared that perhaps social forces were moving in the direction of assimilation, despite government policies to influence it in either direction, and despite contradictory evidence indicating both assimilation and the maintenance of a separate ethnic identity.

However, since my visit occurred just before the fall of the Gang of Four, the situation may have changed. Many observations since that time have indicated that this is indeed the case. It has been my aim to report as accurately as possible the effects of political upheavals on Koreans living in Yenpien, and I hope that in some way what I have been able to observe will be of benefit to others.

# Research Notes

## Notes and Questions Concerning the *Samguk Sagi*'s Chronology of Paekche's Kings Chŏnji, Kuisin, and Piyu

THE final years of the fourth century and the opening decades of the fifth constituted one of the most tumultuous periods in Paekche's history: the kingdom's very existence was first threatened by the onslaught of Koguryŏ's armies, and then its political sovereignty was jeopardized by its consequential reliance on military assistance from Japan. For the most part, Kim Pu-sik's recounting of the events of these troubled years in the *Samguk sagi* is compatible with the information found in other early sources concerned with this period, most importantly the inscription on the memorial stele of King Kwanggaet'o, the pertinent dynastic histories of China, and the *Nihon shoki*. Certain entries from the Chinese and Japanese sources do, however, raise significant doubts about the reliability of the *Samguk sagi*'s dating for the reigns of three of Paekche's early fifth-century rulers: King Chŏnji, King Kuisin, and King Piyu. To articulate these questions clearly, as well as to explicate the solutions offered herein, it will be necessary to open our discussion with a survey of the relevant passages of the *Samguk sagi,* the *Chin shu,* the *Sung shu,* and the *Nihon shoki.*

King Chŏnji, at least according to the *Samguk sagi*'s account, shares with only one other king of Paekche the dubious distinction of having risen to the throne through the intervention of the Japanese government

AUTHOR'S NOTE: As used here, the terms "Japan" and "Japanese" are simplifications that refer to the government and inhabitants of the state which, at the time that concerns us, centered in the Yamato region of the island of Honshū in the Japanese archipelago. While recognizing that the use of these particular terms is historically problematic, the justification of a more precise terminology would raise complex issues extraneous to the present discussion.

after having spent a period of time as a hostage in Japan.[1] Chŏnji was the eldest of the three sons of King Asin (392–405), and, after having been designated the heir apparent in 394, was sent by his father as a hostage to the Japanese court in 397.[2] At the time of his father's death eight years later (405), Chŏnji was still being detained in Japan. In Chŏnji's absence, his youngest brother, Chŏmnye, seized the crown for himself after slaying King Asin's second son, who had established a temporary caretaker government to maintain order until the crown prince returned. Once word of Asin's demise reached the archipelago, the king of Japan (Emperor Ōjin) granted Chŏnji permission to return to his homeland and provided him with a bodyguard of one hundred Japanese soldiers. When Chŏnji and his Japanese guard drew nigh to the Paekche capital, Hansŏng, he received word of Chŏmnye's treachery and prudently withdrew to an island in the Yellow Sea until the patriotic citizens of the capital were able to overthrow and slay the usurping fratricide.[3]

Following the drama attending his accession, the remainder of Chŏnji's reign, as described in the *Samguk sagi,* seems quite staid: he visited the royal ancestral shrine, rewarded those of his subjects who had rendered him service during the contest for the throne, maintained the kingdom's defenses along the border with Koguryŏ, and strove to perpetuate Paekche's diplomatic ties with China and especially—as may be readily understood—with Japan. The *Samguk sagi*'s account of Chŏnji's reign concludes with the statement that he died in the third lunar month of the sixteenth year of his rule (mid-April/early May, 420).[4]

In contrast to its relatively substantial treatment of the notable events of Chŏnji's life and reign, the *Samguk sagi* has very little to say of his successor, King Kuisin. All that it records concerning this man whom it credits with having been the nineteenth king of Paekche is that he was Chŏnji's eldest son, that he was born early in his father's reign, that he ascended to the throne following his father's death in 420, and that he himself died in the twelfth lunar month of the eighth year of his reign

---

1. The other such incident admitted by the *Samguk sagi* was the elevation of Prince P'ung to the throne after the T'ang-Silla capture of King Uija in 660. The *Nihon shoki* asserts, however, that three of Paekche's kings were placed on the throne with Japanese support following a term as hostage in Japan. In addition to Chŏnji and P'ung, it claims that King Tongsŏng (479–501) also became monarch in this fashion. Further, the *Nihon shoki* credits Japanese intervention with responsibility for King Chinsa's assumption of the crown of Paekche in 392, although it does not argue that he was ever a hostage at the Japanese court.

2. Kim Pu-sik, *Samguk sagi* (Chōsen-shi Gakkai, Showa 3 ed.) 25 (Asin 3:2), p. 250, and *Samguk sagi* 25 (Asin 6:5), p. 250.

3. For the events surrounding Chŏnji's accession, see *Samguk sagi* 25 (Chŏnji, Introduction), p. 251.

4. For the events of Chŏnji's reign, see *Samguk sagi* 25 (Chŏnji), pp. 251–252.

(January, 428) and was succeeded by King Piyu, who may have been his eldest son but who may also have been a son of King Chŏnji by a concubine.[5]

The interest of Chinese historians in Korea originated during the Han dynasty with the establishment of Chinese colonies in the northern part of the peninsula in the late second century B.C., and it remained vital following the destruction of those colonies and the rise of the independent Korean kingdoms as tributary states of China during the fourth century A.D. The official histories of the Six Dynasties period (220–589) often mention embassies from the three Korean kingdoms in their chronicle sections, and additional summary descriptions of these states and their diplomatic relations are commonly included among the topical essays *(lieh-chuan)* of the histories. It is evident from the similarity to passages from the Chinese histories of many of the *Samguk sagi*'s entries treating relations with China—a similarity often amounting to verbatim duplication—that Kim Pu-sik made extensive use of these works in compiling his history of early Korea.

Throughout the Six Dynasties period, when the Central Kingdom was divided north and south into two or more contending states, Paekche's monarchs virtually ignored the succession of regimes that ruled northern China, sending only one embassy there during the first two hundred years of the kingdom's diplomatic history.[6] In contrast, during these same two centuries Paekche's kings repeatedly dispatched tribute missions to the southern Chinese dynasties, and, in return, were periodically granted imposing titles by the rulers of south China. When recording both the arrival of tribute missions and the distribution of titles, the Chinese histories often mention the name of the Paekche king involved, but the names used in the Chinese texts are not the same as those found in the *Samguk sagi*. This discrepancy has a simple explanation: the names contained in the Chinese sources reflect the official name used by the king while he was on the throne, whereas the names adopted by the *Samguk sagi* are actually posthumous, ritual titles. The official

5. Among the chronicles of the thirty-one kings of Paekche that appear in the *Samguk sagi*, only those of King Saban (traditionally 234) are briefer than those of King Kuisin. The latter are short enough to permit quotation in their entirety:

> King Kuisin. He was the eldest son of King Chŏnji, and when King Chŏnji died he ascended the throne.
> Eighth Year, Winter, twelfth Month. The king died.
>
> —*Samguk sagi* 25 (Kuisin), p. 252

6. This one embassy was sent to the Northern Wei in 472. Only during the brief period between 567 and 589 did Paekche's rulers regularly send missions to the regimes in both northern and southern China.

personal names appearing in the Chinese histories are in most instances preceded by the surname of the Paekche royal family, Puyŏ (Chinese, Fuyü), which is frequently abbreviated to Yŏ.[7] Since, beginning with the reign of King Kŭnch'ogo (346–375), the *Samguk sagi*'s chronology for Paekche is for the most part supported by evidence derived from other early sources, the differences in the kings' names appearing in the Korean and Chinese histories rarely present serious problems. In most cases it is possible simply to substitute the more widely recognized name from the Korean history for the less well-known one appearing in an earlier Chinese account, once one has determined during which king's reign the Chinese date would fall according to the chronology of the *Samguk sagi*. This simple interpolative procedure, however, does not always prove satisfactory.

Paekche's diplomatic relations with the second of the southern dynasties, the Eastern Chin (317–420), had been solidly established prior to King Chŏnji's accession in 405. The *Chin shu* records the arrival of embassies from the kingdom in 372 (the first tribute mission from Paekche to be mentioned in a Chinese history) and 384, and the conferral of titles upon rulers of the kingdom in 372 and 386.[8] The *Samguk sagi*, in addition to noting the events of 372 and 384, avers that an embassy from the kingdom also visited the Eastern Chin court in 373, and that another was dispatched in 379 but failed to reach China due to inclement weather.[9] Given the onset of the turbulent years of the late fourth and early fifth centuries, it is not surprising that the Korean history mentions no further contacts between Paekche and China for over two decades following the mission of 384. According to the *Samguk sagi* it was not until 406 that this period of diplomatic inactivity was brought to an end by King Chŏnji's dispatch of a tribute mission to the Eastern Chin during his second month on the throne.[10] However, no record of this embassy is contained in any of the early Chinese histories, which, after recording the conferral of a title in 386, make no further mention of Paekche until 416.

Nonetheless, the Chinese and the Korean histories are largely in

7. The name Puyŏ (Chinese, Fuyü) was seemingly adopted by the royal family as its surname to glorify its descent from the respected and comparatively ancient Manchurian tribe of the same name.

8. For the missions of 372 and 384, see *Chin shu* (Po-na ed.) 9 (Hsien-an 2:1), p. 56d, and *Chin shu* 9 (T'ai-yüan 9:7), p. 59b. For the titles of 372 and 386, see *Chin shu* 9 (Hsien-an 2:6), p. 57a, and *Chin shu* 9 (T'ai-yüan 11:4), p. 59c.

9. For the *Samguk sagi*'s references to the events of 372 and 384, see *Samguk sagi* 24 (Kŭnch'ogo 27:1), p. 247, and *Samguk sagi* 24 (Ch'imnyu 1:7), p. 248. For the events of 373 and 379, see *Samguk sagi* 24 (Kŭnch'ogo 28:2), p. 247, and *Samguk sagi* 24 (Kŭn'gusu 5:3), p. 248.

10. *Samguk sagi* 25 (Chŏnji 2:2), p. 251.

agreement concerning the affair of 416. The *Sung shu* contains the earliest Chinese account of this event, stating that in the twelfth year of the I-hsü reign period (405–419) the title of "Supreme Commander, General Stationed in the East, and King of Paekche" was bestowed by the Eastern Chin emperor upon one King Yŏng (Chinese, Ying) of Paekche.[11] This is the first of several references to this ruler in the *Sung shu*. The *Samguk sagi*, without naming the king specifically since the entry is included in the chronicles of Chŏnji's reign, simply repeats the title of 416 as it is found in the Chinese source and makes the further assertion that the title was directly conferred upon the king by a special envoy sent from the Eastern Chin court.[12]

But was the King Yŏng of the *Sung shu* account actually the same man as King Chŏnji, as apparently was assumed by Kim Pu-sik when he compiled the *Samguk sagi* in the twelfth century? Evidence derived from earlier Chinese and Japanese sources strongly suggests not only that he was not, but also that King Chŏnji had, in fact, been dead for some time when the Eastern Chin emperor promulgated the honorific title of 416.

In the introduction to the *Samguk sagi*'s account of Chŏnji's reign, it is stated that he was also known by the name Chikchi and that he was called Yŏng in the *Liang shu*.[13] This passage is doubly interesting: first because Chŏnji makes several significant appearances in the *Nihon shoki* in the guise of Chikchi (Japanese, Toki), and secondly because Kim Pu-sik's choice of the *Liang shu*, where King Yŏng is only mentioned once, rather than the *Sung shu*, where he is mentioned on a number of occasions, is somewhat perplexing.

The *Nihon shoki*'s first reference to Chŏnji (Chikchi) occurs in the entry for the eighth year of Emperor Ōjin's reign (397)[14] where it is recorded that during this year King Asin of Paekche sent his son, Chikchi, to be a hostage at court.[15] Both the occurrence and the date correspond perfectly with the account of the *Samguk sagi* which was discussed previously. Further, the Korean history's narration of the events attending Chŏnji's accession following his return from Japan in 405 is largely corroborated by the *Nihon shoki*'s entry for the sixteenth year of Ōjin's

11. *Sung shu* (Po-na ed.) 97 (*lieh-chuan* 57, Paichi), p. 1349b. King Yŏng is mentioned specifically in this entry.
12. *Samguk sagi* 25 (Chŏnji 12), p. 252.
13. *Samguk sagi* 25 (Chŏnji, Introduction), p. 251. For the *Liang shu* entry that Kim Pu-sik is evidently making reference to, see note 19 below.
14. According to the traditional chronology of the *Nihon shoki* this date would be equivalent to 277 A.D. in the Western system, but if one follows the accepted practice of adding 120 years to the dates appearing in this portion of the text, the result is 397.
15. *Nihon shoki*, 2 vols., Nihon koten bungaku taikei vols. 67, 68 (Tokyo: Showa 40–42 [1965–1967]), 10 (Ōjin 8:3) 1:367. See also W. G. Aston, trans., *Nihongi*, 2 vols. (London: 1896) 1:257.

reign (405).[16] In view of the influence which Japan exercised in Paekche at this time and given the subsequent history of close relations between the two countries, it is not extraordinary that the *Nihon shoki* should contain such reliable and detailed information about the Korean kingdom. Yet having noted the concurrence of the *Samguk sagi*'s and the *Nihon shoki*'s presentation of the basic facts relating to Chŏnji's biography in 397 and 405, it comes as something of a surprise to discover that the Japanese source dates Chŏnji's death and the accession of his successor, Kuisin, to 414, some six years earlier than the date of 420 given by the *Samguk sagi*.[17] Since the *Nihon shoki* also contains one subsequent entry relating to Chŏnji that is dated to Ōjin's thirty-ninth year on the throne (428),[18] which is fourteen years after it had accounted him dead, one might be tempted to dismiss both its notices of 414 and 428 as misplaced and muddled. Yet, while these criticisms clearly apply to the latter entry, information from Chinese sources demonstrates that the *Nihon shoki*'s date of 414 for Chŏnji's death cannot be so readily discounted.

The *Samguk sagi,* it will be recalled, contains the statement in its introduction to the chronicles of King Chŏnji's reign that he is referred to as Yŏng in the *Liang shu*. And indeed the *Liang shu* does record that King Yŏng of Paekche sent tribute consisting of prisoners of war to the Eastern Chin during the I-shü reign period (405–419).[19] The *Sung shu* contains, by contrast, four specific references to King Yŏng as well as two other entries which, as is apparent from their context, also pertain to him. These same six passages were subsequently incorporated in the *Nan shih,* a text to which Kim Pu-sik seemingly alludes elsewhere in the *Samguk sagi.*[20]

The first of the *Sung shu*'s references to King Yŏng concerns the title

16. *Nihon shoki* 10 (Ōjin 16) 1:373; Aston, *Nihongi,* 1:262–263.

17. *Nihon shoki* 10 (Ōjin 25) 1:377; Aston, *Nihongi,* 1:267–268.

18. *Nihon shoki* 10 (Ōjin 39:2) 1:379; Aston, *Nihongi,* 1:270.

19. *Liang shu* (Po-na ed.) 54 (*lieh-chuan* 48, Paichi), p. 453a. While this passage in the *Liang shu* uses the name of King Yŏng, it is possible that Kim Pu-sik got the idea of the identity of King Yŏng and King Chŏnji from the *T'ung tien,* which he quotes widely and expressly in the *Samguk sagi.* In the *T'ung tien*'s description of Paekche, it is said that during the I-hsü reign period (405–419) the title of "Commander of Paekche's Armies" was bestowed upon Paekche's King Chŏn (Chinese, T'ien) by the Eastern Chin emperor. See *T'ung tien* (Taipei 1958–59 edition of the *Shih t'ung*) 185 (Pien-fang 1, Paichi), p. 988a. Since the graph with which Chŏn is written in the *T'ung tien* is the first graph in the *Samguk sagi*'s name of Chŏnji, it is possible that Kim Pu-sik assumed that they referred to the same individual.

20. *Samguk sagi* 13 (Yurimyŏng 31), p. 151. Although Kim Pu-sik makes this oblique reference to the *Nan shih,* I have discovered no substantive textual evidence that he actually used it as a source, whereas his reliance on the *Pei shih* is both extensive and acknowledged. His access to the *Sung shu* is also questionable: of the thirteen instances of diplomatic contact with Paekche found in this Chinese text, he mentions but four, and of the at least

given him by the Eastern Chin emperor in 416. As intimated in our previous discussion of this particular passage, it constitutes the only instance, other than the *Liang shu* account of tribute just noted, in which King Yŏng is mentioned in relation to the Eastern Chin dynasty by a Chinese source. It may be recalled that in the *Samguk sagi,* however, the claim is made that King Chŏnji had sent tribute to this southern dynasty in 406, some ten years before he is said to have received the title of 416. If Kim Pu-sik's account is accurate in these two details, then the conditions under which the title of 416 was promulgated are unique among the eighteen instances in the kingdom's history when its rulers were the recipients of lengthy, formal titles from Chinese emperors.

An examination of these eighteen cases as they are reported in the Chinese histories reveals that such titles were presented to the kings of Paekche in only three situations: (1) when a new dynasty arose in China; (2) when a Chinese emperor received word of the accession of a new king in Paekche; or (3) when the first tribute mission sent by a particular king of Paekche arrived in China. In the ten instances in which the last of these patterns prevailed, the greatest interval separating the arrival of a king's first embassy and the subsequent conferral of a title was three years,[21] and in eight of these cases the interval amounted to less than a year. Accordingly, the *Samguk sagi*'s assertion that ten years intervened between Chŏnji's initial tribute mission of 406 and the previously mentioned presentation of the Eastern Chin title of 416 raises suspicions that either the mission did not occur or that the title was granted, not to Chŏnji, but to a king recently ascended to the throne of Paekche (that is, the second of the patterns just listed). It is possible, and even likely, that both of these suspicions are justified: the embassy of 406 is not mentioned in any Chinese source, and the subsequent references to King Yŏng in the *Sung shu* suggest that Chŏnji, as related in the *Nihon shoki,* must have been dead in 416.

---

twenty-one references concerning the dynasty's relations with Koguryŏ contained in the *Sung shu,* he repeats but three. The mystery is from whence did he get the small number of these references that he does incorporate in the *Samguk sagi?* If they were borrowed from the *Sung shu,* or the derivative portions of the *Nan shih,* then why were they chosen and the rest ignored? He rarely exhibited a similar degree of selectivity in borrowing from Chinese histories. For example, the *Samguk sagi* repeats twenty-seven of the twenty-nine references in the *Wei shu* to diplomatic contacts between Koguryŏ and the Northern Wei court during the period of primary concern to the *Sung shu,* that is, 420–479. Most of these twenty-seven passages in the *Samguk sagi* constitute verbatim and uncredited quotes from the *Wei shu.*

21. These three-year intervals occurred during the Northern Ch'i and T'ang periods, and in both instances the delay in the conferral of the title followed Paekche's belated sending of its first embassies to the dynasties involved. Paekche's first embassy to the Northern Ch'i arrived in 567 and the title was conferred in 570; the kingdom's first embassy to the T'ang arrived in 621 and the title was conferred in 624.

It is recorded in the *Sung shu* that in the same year that the Liu Sung dynasty was established (420), its founder proclaimed that King Yŏng of Paekche should be awarded a somewhat grander version of the title granted him four years earlier by the preceding Eastern Chin dynasty. By the terms of the decree of 420, King Yŏng was promoted from "General Stationed in the East" to "Great General Stationed in the East."[22] As a similar promotion was simultaneously granted to Koguryŏ's King Nyŏn (Chinese, Lien=King Changsu, 413–491), and as neither Korean monarch had yet sent tribute to the Liu Sung court, it is evident that the generosity of the founder of the new dynasty was mainly intended to manifest his authority over the tributary states of the vanquished Eastern Chin.

Notwithstanding the honor done King Yŏng in 420, it was not until 424 by the *Sung shu*'s acount that he sent tribute to the Liu Sung.[23] This visit of Paekche's first tribute mission to the new southern dynasty seemingly elicited the even greater honor that proceeded from the Liu Sung emperor in the following year (425) when a Chinese ambassador was sent to Paekche to convey an imperial commendation for the king's loyal behavior and to invest him formally in the title that had been proclaimed in 420.[24] According to the account of the Chinese histories, this was the first time that an envoy from China visited Paekche.[25] In spite of this notable event in the history of the kingdom, it was not until 429, some four years after the visit of the Chinese ambassador, that the second embassy from Paekche reached the Liu Sung court.[26] The *Sung shu*'s final reference to King Yŏng is the statement that he was granted a posthumous title when, in 430, King Pi (Chinese, P'i=King Piyu) renewed the kingdom's ongoing diplomatic association with the Liu Sung by sending tribute.[27] Appar-

22. *Sung shu* 3 (Yung-ch'u 1:7), p. 42c. King Yŏng is mentioned specifically in this entry. For a fuller accounting of the titles granted to the rulers of Paekche and Koguryŏ in 420, see *Sung shu* 97 (*lieh-chuan* 57, Kaochüli), p. 1348d. The *Samguk sagi* mentions neither title.

23. *Sung shu* 97 (*lieh-chuan* 57, Paichi), p. 1349d. King Yŏng is mentioned specifically in this entry, as is the name of the Paekche envoy. The *Samguk sagi* contains no reference to this tribute mission.

24. *Sung shu* 97 (*lieh-chuan* 57, Paichi), p. 1349d. Neither this embassy nor the presentation of the title is mentioned in the *Samguk sagi*.

25. As mentioned previously in the text, however, the *Samguk sagi* claims that the title of 416 was personally delivered by an Eastern Chin ambassador. Given the near identity of the Eastern Chin and the Liu Sung titles, is it possible that Kim Pu-sik simply applied some of the information regarding the title of 425 to the title of 416?

26. *Sung shu* 5 (Yüan-chia 6:7), p. 53a. This tribute mission of 429 is mentioned in the *Samguk sagi,* but is credited to King Piyu whose reign the Korean history dates from 428 to 455. See *Samguk sagi* 25 (Piyu 3), p. 252.

27. *Sung shu* 97 (*lieh-chuan* 57, Paichi), pp. 1349d–1350a. King Yŏng is mentioned specifically in this entry. The *Samguk sagi* mentions both the tribute and the posthumous title, but claims that the latter was bestowed directly by an envoy sent from the Liu Sung court. See *Samguk sagi* 25 (Piyu 4:4), p. 252.

ently, King Yŏng had died during the brief period separating the dispatch of his embassy of 429 and the arrival in the following year of the mission sent by King Piyu.[28]

The passages of the *Sung shu* which have just been cited make it obvious that Kim Pu-sik was not correct in either his identification of King Yŏng with King Chŏnji or his assertion that King Chŏnji died in 420. The *Sung shu*'s references to King Yŏng span the period between 416 and 430, and moreover they reveal that the monarch whom a visiting Chinese ambassador knew as King Yŏng was alive and well enough in 425 to personally receive investiture in the title that the Liu Sung emperor had awarded him *in absentia* five years earlier. Since this King Yŏng was already on the throne in 416 and his rule continued without interruption until 429 or 430, it is clear that the *Samguk sagi*'s dating of the end of Chŏnji's reign and the start of Kuisin's stands in need of revision. In this context, the *Nihon shoki*'s record of Chŏnji's death and Kuisin's enthronement takes on added significance. Both the Chinese and the Japanese sources concur in the view that there was a recently crowned king on the throne of Paekche in 416, a ruler known to the *Sung shu* and other Chinese histories as King Yŏng and to the *Nihon shoki*—and the *Samguk sagi*—as King Kuisin.

Concerning the reign of King Kuisin's successor, King Piyu, there is both less cause, and, as the *Nihon shoki* contains no references to him at all, less basis for debate. While the *Samguk sagi* places Piyu's accession at 428, it is evident from the earlier and more extensive records of the *Sung shu* that he ascended the throne following King Kuisin's death in 429/430. The *Samguk sagi*'s date of 455 for his death, however, is generally supported by the *Sung shu,* where it is recorded that the last of four embassies from Piyu arrived at the Liu Sung court in 450, and that the next tribute mission from Paekche, which arrived in 457, was sent by his son and successor, King Kae (Chinese, Ch'ing=King Kaero, 455– 475).[29]

28. The *Sung shu* records that the mission of 429 arrived in the seventh lunar month of the sixth year of the Yüan-chia reign period (late August/early September, 429). The Chinese history gives no more specific date than the reign year for the arrival of the mission of 430, but the *Samguk sagi* dates this mission to the fourth lunar month of Yüan-chia 7 (mid-May/early June, 430). It is interesting to note that the Korean history does date Kuisin's death to the twelfth lunar month, which would fall between these two dates, but of course the *Samguk sagi* places Kuisin's death in an entirely different year, namely 428 (the twelfth lunar month of Yüan-chia 4). Attention should also be drawn to the fact that many histories of Korea written in the twentieth century misinterpret the year of Kuisin's death as given in the *Samguk sagi* as being equivalent to 427 of the western calendar. Actually, the twelfth lunar month of Yüan-chia 4 is equivalent to January, 428.

29. For the mission of 450, see *Sung shu* 5 (Yüan-chia 27:1), p. 63c; and for that of 457, see *Sung shu* 6 (Ta-ming 1:10), p. 73d. For additional references to both missions, see *Sung shu* 97 (*lieh-chuan* 57, Paichi), p. 1350a. Neither the mission of 450 nor that of 457 is mentioned in the *Samguk sagi*.

These entries from the *Sung shu* demonstrate that Piyu must have died sometime during the interval between 450 and 457, a conclusion which accords with the *Samguk sagi*'s date of 455.

The history of Paekche during the late fourth and early fifth centuries as related in the *Samguk sagi* is largely substantiated by the accounts of the early Chinese and Japanese sources. As has been shown, however, evidence from the Chinese and Japanese histories makes it apparent that the *Samguk sagi*'s chronology for the reigns of three early fifth-century kings of Paekche is not entirely trustworthy. Information extracted from the *Sung shu* and the *Nihon shoki,* in particular, argues forcefully that the *Samguk sagi*'s dates of 405–420 for King Chŏnji's reign should be revised to 405–414, that its dates of 420–428 for King Kuisin's reign should be revised to 414–429/430, and that its dates of 428–455 for King Piyu's reign should be revised to 429/430–455.

Jonathan W. Best
Wesleyan University

# Book Reviews

*Celebration of Continuity: Themes in Classic East Asian Poetry.* Peter
H. Lee. Cambridge: Harvard University Press, 1979. viii, 264 pp.
$17.50.

Professor Lee's purpose in this study is to set forth the pervasive topical conventions of East Asian poetry, to set them forth and to show how they have been
made to function in particular instances, framed by local cultural needs and individual poetic intention. Such a purpose might suggest for its product an extensive
catalog of topics with an adequate sprinkling of examples of the various usages.
But that is not what the author is after. He has a more serious intention. He
wants to teach us how to read East Asian poetry as it was meant to be read. His
method: through a study of their topical conventions, to bring us closer to the
poems as they might have been experienced by their intended audience. In this he
is assuming that poems are composed more out of poetry than experience, particularly in conservative cultures. It is by understanding the accumulated and ac-
cumulating meanings drawn to themselves by common topics that we can better
understand the function of a given topic in any of its particular usages. We can,
that is, see a particular usage against a background of general usages and judge
whether the poet, however artfully, has merely echoed (and thus reenforced)
some conventional meaning in a topic or has found a new possibility in it. We
can thus respond with more precision to particular poetic intentions. To quote
him:

Such study should not only discover and classify the conscious use of literary "constants," but try to account for the contextual functions, the qualitative distinctions, and
the individual use to which these constants are put. (p. 2)

A conventional river passes through many East Asian poems, but it is always
more or less compelled to take on the contours imposed by the local landscape of
the individual poem. Night, as a topic, is full of possibilities gathered over centuries of poetic usage. It will not do simply to include these in a catalog of topics
and their meanings. The particular meaning of a convention in any poem derives

from a knowledge shared by poet and audience. Professor Lee has attempted to create the sense of the poetic culture which made that knowledge an active principle in its literary experience. It is this that makes the book so richly valuable to modern readers, especially those with no immediate feel for the value of the conventions of Chinese, Japanese, and Korean poetry.

Professor Lee, to bring this immense subject into some sort of order, has divided the great and persistent themes in East Asian poetry into a pentad: praise, nature, love, friendship, and time. And he has listed the important topics that have gathered to each of these. But this much—which is considerable—does not make for the value of the study. What does that is his fine discriminations respecting conventional usage. Clifford Geertz, discussing cultural theory, asserts that "What generality it contrives to achieve grows out of the delicacy of its distinctions, not the sweep of its abstractions." This could as well apply to Professor Lee's approach, especially the word "delicacy." Particularly for the western reader who knows none of the languages of the literatures under discussion, delicacy makes all the difference. The fineness of perception always seems based on a richly detailed sense of the materials, on examples chosen because they are representative, not because they conveniently illustrate a position.

Professor Lee does not confine himself to East Asian examples in his attempt to illuminate his subject. His method is avowedly comparative. He uses western poetry as a sort of sustained analog to provide a ready means of comparison and contrast for an English-speaking audience. This procedure is, of course, enormously helpful. But such is his command over the tradition of western poetry that we receive an extra, perhaps unintended, benefit: we see poetry of our own tradition in a fresh light, as—among other things—a field of conventions that operate as they do in Asian poetry, as a vast store of possibilities which individual poets select from to render a particular intention. This surely is not a new way of seeing western poetry, but it serves to remind us what we are easily apt to forget: how much individual poetic voice or style is a matter of playing with available conventional possibilities. In this light, tradition is to be perceived as a mass of golden opportunities, not, as it has been perceived from the Romantics on, as a barrier to fresh perception. Of course it can be that, but, as East Asian poetry shows, it can be the very reverse. It can be a broad way through the wilderness of experience. That is a tonic notion for those of us raised on current aesthetic dogma—about all, that to the degree which poetry exploits convention it is inauthentic. The fact that any poem, insofar as it claims to be a poem, exploits convention does not seem to make much difference to Romantic criticism and practice. Perhaps over the long haul such studies as Professor Lee's will make a difference. We sometimes see what is nearby more clearly by seeing it through what seems to be a strange or even alien medium.

There is little to add to all this except to say that Professor Lee's prose is always lucid and strong. While I am in no position to judge the faithfulness of the translations of the East Asian poetry, it can be said that they are never less than serviceable.

Perhaps it would be good to conclude with a passage from *Celebrations* (pp. 148–149), one which exhibits Professor Lee's comparative procedure where we see both the way topics are used within one tradition, in two related traditions and, by way of contrast, how they are used in the West:

The times depicted for parting are often conventionally given as autumn and winter, the seasons of decay and death, but the chilly sky and water do not deter the traveler. The anguish of the speaker is mirrored by nature, which mirrors his state of mind:

> The river darkens, rain about to fall;
> Waves turn white as the wind comes up.

Ho Sun (d. 518)

> The birds' anguished cry in the north wind—

Lang Shih-yuan

The following poem by Yi Chŏng-bo (1693–1766) succinctly offers the reason for the tearful parting in autumn:

> Man's greatest sorrow is the sorrow of parting
> That wrenches our soul.
> Among tall sweet grasses and green willows,
> Parting on a long bridge
> Darkens your heart.
> When a goose cries and fallen leaves sough,
> Who won't shed tears at my song?

The solitary boat "becomes one with the blue sky," says Li Po in "Seeing Meng Hao-jan Off to Kuang-ling": "Now, only the Long River flowing to the sky's end." Chong Chi-sang (d. 1135) says his tears are sources of the Taedong River:

> After a rain on the long dike grasses are thick.
> With a sad song I send you off to Namp'o.
> When will the Taedong River cease to flow?
> Year after year my tears will swell the waves.

As in love lyrics, the sea or river is separation, and "the endless white clouds"—dark or drifting clouds or steep mountains elsewhere—are another symbol to underscore the vastness of distance and the enormity of sorrow. The ship might on occasion suggest the ship of life that braves, for example, "Rockes, or Remoraes" (Donne's "To Sir Henry Wotton"), but seldom, as far as I know, is it employed in Korea as a metaphor of the ship of poetry, with poetic efforts likened to sailing.

Leonard Nathan<br>University of California, Berkeley

## A Second View of Peter H. Lee's *Celebration of Continuity*

Most Japanese scholars would readily acknowledge the profound indebtedness of their classical poetry to the literatures of the rest of East Asia, but few have made a comprehensive study of the subject. The reason is not so much a linguistic one, because every specialist in early Japanese verse is expected to be competent in classical Chinese. It has more to do with methodology, or the lack of it, for by and large comparative literature in Japan has meant a study of Japanese and Western literatures. With a few exceptions, studies that compare Japanese and other East Asian literatures have been rare, and the exceptions that do exist are largely confined to historical topics.

Peter H. Lee's *Celebration of Continuity* is a valuable pioneering work in this field, because it not only offers a number of significant insights into East Asian poetry as a collective unit but also provides a methodological point of departure for future scholars who might want to venture into this area of study. Students of Japanese literature, myself among them, have not really made a serious attempt to go beyond the national borders and identify prominent themes common to Chinese, Korean and Japanese poetry in premodern times. Professor Lee has done just that; he has identified praise, nature, love, friendship, and time as five such themes. To many students of Japanese literature, again including myself, the inclusion of praise and friendship come as a revelation, because, as Professor Lee himself has noted, there were very few Japanese poems on these two subjects. The book offers many other insights which are equally enlightening about the general nature of East Asian poetry. To cite several more examples, the author notes that imitation was not the aim of East Asian nature poetry, for "the mimetic theory was nonexistent in East Asia" (p. 60). On another occasion he intimates that "there is probably more poetry on friendship than on love in China and Korea" (p. 144). And elsewhere he refers to the East Asian concept of history and observes: ". . . where history is viewed as recurrence, not as development with a clear end, such a world-view is bound to affect the development of narrative as well" (p. 212). Whenever a student of Japanese literature comes across such and other observations on East Asian poetry, he will stop, as I did, to ponder the issue in the context of Japanese poetry, and that will lead him to avenues of thought he has never trodden before.

The book includes instances of discontinuity, as well as continuity, of Japanese poetry within the East Asian literary tradition. As already mentioned, the Japanese wrote very few poems on praise or friendship. On the other hand they produced a great number of verses on love, and if love lyrics occupy only a "minor place" in the poetical hierarchy of China and Korea as Professor Lee says (p. 142), the Japanese made a radical departure from the central tradition. As for the theme of time, Professor Lee writes that East Asian poets tried to transcend time by their faith in poetry, but I am inclined to believe that Japanese poets in general had considerably less faith in their art. Some of them even feared that their faith in poetry might prevent them from attaining a higher level of religious enlightenment.

The book covers an enormously wide range of materials both historically and geographically, a task that could have been undertaken only by a scholar with the erudition and linguistic versatility of Professor Lee. But there is one area of East Asian poetry which is almost entirely omitted from the book and which I dearly miss: Japanese haiku. I am curious to know the reasons for the omission, because two of the most influential poets in the genre, Bashō and Buson, had great respect for classical Chinese literature, and their works clearly show that. I do not believe, however, that the inclusion of haiku in the discussions would have affected the validity of Professor Lee's contentions as they now stand. On the contrary, I think it would have strengthened his arguments.

All in all, I think Professor Lee has admirably attained the goal he set out to reach: the identification and analysis of major themes in East Asian literature. Now the next step is up to all of us in East Asian literature, and that step would be to study the particularizations of each theme by a nation, by a period, or by a specific poet, and to seek out the reasons for the vicissitudes. Why didn't the Japanese produce more encomiastic poetry? What accounts for their failure to write more poems presenting fishermen as sages? These and many other questions, raised in the book explicitly and implicitly, wait for an answer from a student of Japanese literature. We owe much to Professor Lee not only for raising these questions but also for providing a general framework within which to answer them.

Makoto Ueda<br>
Stanford University

*The Korean Diaspora: Historical and Sociological Studies of Korean Immigration and Assimilation in North America.* Edited by Hyung-chan Kim. Santa Barbara, California: American Bibliographical Center (Clio Press), 1978. xi, 268 pp. Index. Hardcover edition $19.75.

It is encouraging to see a growing academic interest in overseas Koreans. After all, Koreans comprise one of the largest ethnic categories world-wide, and the increasing migration of Koreans deserves the attention of both Korean specialists and social scientists. This little collection of essays, edited by Hyung-chan Kim, is to my knowledge the first volume devoted to historical and social-scientific studies of Koreans in America, and for that reason alone merits our attention.

Unfortunately, this is a book which can be recommended only with some serious reservations, the first of which has to do with its title and ostensible goals. It seems to me that "diaspora," while technically a correct term for Korean migration abroad, is so clearly identified with the forcible dispersion of Jews that it obscures the Korean case. It is true that the Japanese promoted Korean labor migration in Asia, but Korean migration to the United States, with which this book concerns itself, has little in common with the Jewish experience. This is a problem in part because the book's editor suggests that one of the major purposes of the collection is to investigate the "uniqueness" of the Korean experience in America. Why a social scientist should wish to establish uniqueness is beyond my comprehension, since to some extent every ethnic minority has had a "unique" experience, and for that matter so has every individual, regardless of ethnicity. I should think that "understanding" would have been a happier choice of goals for the book, but in any case the quest for uniqueness is not well served by an implicit comparison with Jews, which the title certainly suggests.

Whether intentional or not, the search for uniqueness seems to have had a deleterious effect upon this book in that there are precious few references to the voluminous historical and social-scientific literature on assimilation of other ethnic minorities into American society. One paper by Chae-kŭn Yu, on personality adjustment of Korean children, does build itself upon Gordon's *Assimilation in American Life,* and the editor's paper on business enterprise examines

Ivan Light's contention that the Asian success story in business is related to self-help organizations (in the case of Koreans, the *kye*). But nowhere is the Korean experience explicitly compared with other immigrant categories, and aside from a few oblique references to Chinese and Japanese, the average reader will find oneself in a vacuum. In several papers dealing with assimilation and acculturation, one finds references to hardship, underemployment, business failures and successes, but without some basis for comparison, the reader cannot evaluate the Korean experience. It is well known that all immigrant groups to the United States have experienced deprivation relative to the host society for one or more generations. The real question here is, how have Koreans succeeded as compared to other Americans? (We all are migrants or descendants of migrants, after all.) This volume does not begin to answer that question, and I believe that the failure to address comparative questions is a serious weakness, from either a Korean or American point of view, or from the standpoint of either an academician or layman.

On a more positive note, *The Korean Diaspora* does present some valuable information on Koreans in the United States. The editor's papers on social demography and ethnic business enterprises are both useful contributions. Marn J. Cha's paper on political orientation and assimilation, Jai P. Ryu's demographic analysis, and a paper on business development in Los Angeles by David Kim and Charles Wong all present original and valuable data. Other papers in the volume vary from excellent to poor.

Wayne Patterson presents an account of the first attempts to bring Korean plantation laborers to Hawaii. Data on the subject are very scarce, so the author is understandably required to introduce conjecture at various points. However, he becomes so engrossed in the question of who might have said or done what, that the essay begins to read like an Arthur-Conan-Doyle mystery. An actual account of the early immigration itself is taken up by Yŏ-jun Yun, with an interesting comparison of the experiences of Koreans in the U.S. and in Mexico.

Hyung-chan Kim contributed two more papers in addition to those mentioned previously. They address themselves to the role of the Christian church (in Hawaii, largely) and of community organizations (mostly the mainland) in Korean adaptation. The papers are largely historical, except for a rather gossipy discussion of recent problems in community organizations in California. Neither approach the quality of the other two chapters by the same author.

Three more papers included in the volume are most specifically oriented to social-scientific concerns. One on communication and acculturation, by Won H. Chang, produces some interesting relationships between three sets of value orientations and reactions to communication with Americans. Unfortunately, the conclusions rest upon a very small sample of thirty cases, so the rather complex hypotheses and analyses become more interesting than the results. Small samples also weaken an otherwise potentially important network study of two different Korean communities by Don-chang Lee. In addition, the relationships between research methods and data are not made very clear in Lee's contribution, which might lead to some questions about his conclusions. Chae-kŭn Yu examines some correlates of cultural assimilation in a study of 238 Korean families in Washington state. This paper is seriously weakened by oversimplistic data analysis (among other things, Pearson's C is not a very good choice for correlation analysis), and, although the subject matter of Yu's chapter is important, the results are not very convincing.

The book ends with an excellent summary of source materials on Korean immigrants to the United States by Arthur L. Gardner. This may be, in time, the most valuable contribution of the volume. Hyung-chan Kim's editorial contributions are clear and he gives succinct summaries of the various chapters, but little or no attempt is made to pull the whole together.

In all, this volume is important as source material for students of Korean assimilation, and may be of interest to Korean immigrants. However, the uneven quality of various contributions, plus the failure to place the Korean experience in some relevant context, lead me to recommend it only to those seriously involved in the study of Korean assimilation, and then with reservations.

Herbert R. Barringer
University of Hawaii

*The Gold-Crowned Jesus and Other Writings.* By Kim Chi Ha. Edited by Chong Sun Kim and Shelly Killen. Illustrated by George Knowlton. Maryknoll, New York: Orbis Books, 1978. 1?1 pp. $5.95.

Who is Kim Chi Ha? In this long-needed anthology, historian Chong Sun Kim, prison art scholar Shelly Killen, artist George Knowlton, translation assistant Winifred Caldwell, translators of the Japanese Council for Justice and Peace, and the staff of the publishing house of the Catholic Foreign Mission Society of America (Maryknoll) have combined their talents to help the English-reading world find out.

In the preface the editors insightfully introduce Kim's life and works, partly by comparison with Camus, Dostoevsky, and Tolstoy, but with emphasis on Kim's Korean cultural roots. They conclude that as "a charismatic figure who uses the forms of shaman incantations and rich Korean colloquialisms in his poetry, Kim is the only Asian poet to combine the essence of Christian socialism with his native tradition" (p. xiii). Fair enough, but perhaps Kim, who resists labeling, would not find even this completely comfortable. "I hate to stick things within the confines of a certain defined framework" (p. 50).

The interpretive preface is followed by a biographical chronology: Born Kim Yongil in Mokp'o on February 4, 1941, Kim Chi Ha participated in the 1960 student movement, opposed the normalization of Korean-Japanese relations in 1964 and 1965, and has been a poet-playwright critic of poverty, corruption, dictatorship, and torture since 1969. In 1971 he was active in the Farmer's Cooperative Movement, which was led by the Catholic church, and he also organized several hundred Catholics in a demonstration for the realization of social justice (Kim formally converted to Catholicism in 1973). Condemned to death on July

13, 1974, his sentence was commuted to life imprisonment on July 20; and he was suddenly released from prison on February 15, 1975. Rearrested on March 13, 1975, after the publication of his prison diary, *Torture Road,* he was tortured into admitting he was a communist on March 20. In response, Kim smuggled out an explanation of his true beliefs, a "Declaration of Conscience," on August 4. Seven years were added to his original life sentence in December, 1976. The chronology just outlined ends with 1977, however, it should be added that Kim's sentence was reduced to twenty years on December 27, 1978, in a presidential amnesty that freed 5,378 other prisoners.

In the remainder of the book Kim speaks for himself in poems, "Prayer," "Mount Chiri," "Seoul," "The Road," and "The Rope Walker"; in his "Declaration of Conscience" (1975); in religious testimony, a letter to the National Priests Association for the Realization of Justice (1975); in excerpts from his court interrogation (1976); in an abridgement of his final statement in court (1976); in the prose-poem "Torture Road—1974"; and finally in the play *The Gold-Crowned Jesus* (date not clear), whose main characters are a leper, a beggar, a prostitute, a businessman, a policeman, a priest, a nun, and Jesus.

Kim speaks best for himself. As poet, political prisoner, and playwright he reveals himself to be an enormously gifted pearl, constantly perfecting human potential amidst unspeakable and needless repression. He is a political artist in the process of creation:

I stand on my human right to be creative [p. 26]. . . . My ideological education is incomplete [p. 18]. . . . I believe that the truth, only the truth, will liberate people [p. 20]. . . . I want a victory for real democracy, complete freedom of speech [p. 20]. . . . There is no democracy as long as the people cannot depose an undesirable ruler [p. 20]. . . . Even granting the importance of national security, only the unity of the people assures it. And democracy is a prerequisite for unity [p. 43]. . . . The revolution I support will be a synthesis of true nonviolence and an agonized violence of love [p. 22]. . . . That revolution will not follow foreign models or patterns, but flow from our unique revolutionary tradition [p. 23]. . . . I believe in a wide sense that Christianity is a revolutionary religion [p. 52]. . . . A Christian revolution is the apocalyptic vision of the mass resurrection of the people [p. 52]. . . . By making the poor the heroes of my works and having them gain victory, I was trying to express the possibility of salvation [p. 56]. . . . I believe therefore that we must put the poor in the center of the movement [p. 57]. . . . When the resentment of the people turns into blind violence, the result is a horror. Here the Christian philosophy of nonviolence, and its teaching of love, must be mobilized to awaken the people's consciousness [p. 63]. . . . I am not a Communist. My opposition to oppression and exploitation aren't because I am a Communist but because I am a radical Catholic [p. 42]. . . . The disintegration of dictatorship in both the north and the south is inevitable [p. 64].

The editors of *The Gold-Crowned Jesus and Other Writings* have placed Kim Chi Ha's figure solidly before readers of the English language just as Kim has placed the figures of the poor and violated before the consciences of Korea and the world. Ignorance is no longer excusable in scholarly circles. As long as the pen of poet Kim is silenced, no one is truly free.

Glenn D. Paige
University of Hawaii

*An Jū-Kon to Nik-Kan kankeishi* [An Chung-gǔn and the History of Japanese-Korean Relations]. By Ichikawa Seimei. Tokyo: Hara Shobō, 1979. 675 pp. ¥5,000.

In April 1979, the chief of staff of the Japanese Land Self-Defense Forces visited South Korea, and the Korean-Japanese Parliamentary Conference on Security Affairs was established. In July, the Director-General of the Japanese Defense Agency paid his first official visit. There is no doubt that Japanese-South Korean relations entered a new epoch. Japanese companies already own 58 percent of all foreign equity in South Korea, and South Korea is heavily dependent upon Japanese trade.

In spite of such close ties between Japan and South Korea, the two peoples have yet to resolve the emotional conflicts that have persisted since Japan forced the opening of the hermit kingdom in 1876. The interaction between Japan and South Korea since the two nations "normalized" their relations in 1965 has been predominantly economic in character. Intellectual and cultural exchanges have been sporadic and formal. While a great number of Japanese tourists and businessmen have visited South Korea, the contacts between the two peoples have been superficial at best. The two peoples have yet to "touch their hearts." The Koreans could very well sympathize with Mao Tse-tung and Chou En-lai who took strong exception to Premier Tanaka's comment in Peking that Japan had caused "inconveniences" to China in the 1930s and 1940s.

Examples abound. In March 1979, the head of the Japanese Federation of Managerial Organizations (Nihon Keieisha Dantai Rengōkai), Sakurada, caused a major incident at an international seminar by stating that the phenomenal growth of the South Korean economy was due to excellent education provided during the Japanese colonial period. The unanimous reaction of the Korean press was that of anger. They recalled that in March 1955 Kubota Kanichirō, the head of the Japanese delegation in the Korean-Japanese negotiations for the normalization of relations, had stated that the establishment of a former colony as an independent nation before the signing of a treaty of peace was rather unusual; that the United States should be criticized for enforcing complete repatriation of Japanese residents from Korea before a treaty of peace had been concluded; that the Japanese administration of Korea was not altogether bad, and that much was done to help the Koreans in the sense that port facilities, schools, and hospitals were built and spectacular advances were made in rice cultivation; and that the reference in the Cairo Declaration to the Korean people as being in a state of slavery was an exaggeration caused by the emotional stress of war. The Japanese government refused to rescind this so-called Kubota statement for two years in spite of the violent reaction of the Korean government. Both of these remarks have been characterized in Korea as "mangǒn" (bōgen in Japanese) or reckless remarks.

These "incidents" of recent years are worth noting because very similar types of emotional conflict and differences of opinion prevailed in 1909 when Count Ito Hirobumi was assassinated by An Chung-gǔn in Harbin. Ito and his colleagues undoubtedly believed that the Japanese policy of placing Korea under its control was justified for the sakes of both Japan and Korea. Since the early 1890s, Japan had striven without avail to encourage the Korean government to reform itself in order to put the latter on firmer political, economic, and diplomatic grounds. Only by annexing Korea could Korea be reformed and the stability of East Asia be assured. Recalcitrant Koreans, a group including that nation's emperor, should be disposed of for the good of Korea.

The Korean reaction to Japanese policy, however, was quite the opposite. Many Koreans had supported Japan's war efforts against Russia between 1904 and 1905, because of the Japanese declaration that the war was to assure peace in Asia and to consolidate Korea's independence. For racial and cultural reasons, the Koreans also preferred Japan over Russia. Various remarks of An Chung-gŭn to his interrogators also indicate that the Koreans were resigned to Japanese "protection" of Korea in the wake of the Japanese victory against Russia. But as Japan turned Korea into a simple colony by dethroning the Korean emperor, by dissolving the Korean army, by taking over Korea's economy, and by suppressing the Korean people, Koreans felt betrayed. Japan was nothing more than an aggressor to be defied. The rising of the "Righteous Armies" after 1907 attests to this. According to the Japanese Garrison Army's report of 1913, 17,697 Koreans were killed between 1907 and 1911, 3,706 were wounded, and 1,994 captured. (Chōsen Chūtō-gun, Bōtō tōbatsushi [Record of Subjugation of Insurgents], 1913, appendix, tables 2–3.) Since Ito had personally masterminded the conclusion of various treaties and directed Japanese actions in Korea as the first Resident-General in Korea, Ito was blamed as the kingpin of Japanese perfidy and aggression. To the nationalistically minded Koreans, therefore, the assassination of Ito was amply justified. Ito was a villain and An Chung-gŭn was a hero. To the Japanese, however, the assassination was a wanton act of an ignorant recalcitrant.

By and large, these contrasting interpretations, attitudes, and emotions persist even today, seventy years after Ito was assassinated and thirty-five years after Korea was liberated from Japan. Today, An Chung-gŭn is enshrined as a national hero, and his statue stands on a hill in Namsan overlooking Seoul. On the other hand, Ito Hirobumi's picture adorns the thousand-yen bills in Japan. The Japanese and Korean peoples continue to interact with each other without making any attempt to resolve the deep-seated emotional conflict.

Publication of more information about An Chung-gŭn in itself, of course, is not likely to resolve the long-drawn-out emotional conflict. But if anyone hopes to move Japanese-Korean relations beyond the superficial level and build genuine ties of friendship between the two nations, the implications of the assassination must be discussed and understood. In this sense, Professor Ichikawa's volume is an important contribution to the understanding of Japanese-Korean relations, and the eventual resolution of Japanese-Korean conflicts.

Of the many parts of Ichikawa's present volume, the most important are An's autobiography written in prison and the texts of prosecutors' interrogation of An and his accomplices. Other parts of the volume written by Professor Ichikawa are provided as background materials. They include a brief history of Japanese-Korean relations, an account of Korean resistance against Japanese encroachment, brief biographies of Ito and An Chung-gŭn, a description of the assassination, and synopses of foreign reactions toward the incident. Scholars familiar with the existing literature will not make new discoveries from these background materials (pp. 1–208), but most of the relevant materials are conveniently and succinctly presented for both the scholar and the general reader.

As the editor states in his preface, An Chung-gŭn's autobiography had been discovered before, and Ichikawa himself had edited it for publication (*Ito Hirobumi Ansatsu Kiroku,* Tokyo: Hara Shobo, 1972, 737 pp.) But this edition was a Japanese translation written in the style of the late Meiji era. The original text was discovered only recently, and Ichikawa reprinted it in this volume along with a new Japanese translation. The texts of the interrogations supplement the autobiography.

An Chung-gŭn's autobiography was written during a four-month period between December 13, 1909 and March 15, 1910. It not only scans his brief life (1879–1910) and career, but also offers fresh glimpses into the turbulent society in which he lived. An's father was evidently a person of intelligence who had passed various grades of civil service examinations. (An is of two minds about his father serving as the prefectural governor of Chinhae.) In 1884, his father had been selected by Pak Yŏng-hyo, the progressive leader, to be sent to Japan for modern education, but as Pak failed in the coup d'etat of that year, all those close to Pak were arrested and subjected to various degrees of punishment. An's father fled to a mountain village in Hwanghae province and reared his three children. Chung-gŭn did receive his classical education, but was wont to spend his time hunting.

In 1894, when he was fifteen, Chung-gŭn had his first taste of armed combat. As the Tonghaks rose in revolt against the government and ravaged the territory, Chung-gŭn's father mobilized some seventy hunters for the protection of his village and the neighboring area. The Tonghaks sent some 20,000 men, according to An Chung-gŭn, to quash the hunters, but a surprise attack on the enemy's headquarters led to the hunters' victory and enabled them to capture a great quantity of grain, weapons, ammunition, and horses. But the capture of grain led to a prolonged dispute with two of the most powerful royal ministers who claimed ownership. The ministers' persecution led An's father to hide in a Catholic mission operated by a French missionary, who succeeded in converting An's father and his family. The new converts devoted themselves to evangelical work with zeal. For a while, Chung-gŭn studied French and aspired to establish a college.

An Chung-gŭn characterizes the local officials of that era as corrupt and avaricious, and offers a number of vivid examples. As Catholics defied these officials, the officials treated the church with severe enmity, and strove to find excuses to persecute the Catholics. An's father was a marked man, but escaped arrest by hiding again. He became despondent, however, and eventually drank himself to illness. Other Catholics survived only through the protection of the French missionaries. The foreigners, including Chung-gŭn's French priest and the Chinese doctor consulted by An's father, behaved wantonly against the Koreans as well.

Eventually, however, An Chung-gŭn's attention turned toward the Japanese, who, having won the war against Russia, began to take over Korea. An Chung-gŭn at first thought of taking the family abroad, but while he was visiting Shanghai on an exploratory trip, he was dissuaded by a French missionary of old acquaintance and was persuaded to devote himself to education, cultivation of national strength, and the unification of the people. Chung-gŭn established two schools in Chinnamp'o near P'yongyang and engaged in coal mining to acquire funds, but, "facing Japanese obstructions," his venture came to naught. In 1907, when the "Righteous Armies" movement erupted, Chung-gŭn went to Chientao in Manchuria and then to Vladivostok seeking action. An arduous campaign among the Koreans enabled him to organize a band of some three hundred men with whom he attacked a Japanese outpost in Korea in June 1908, but when he released the Japanese prisoners his men captured, his men scattered away. After a long skirmish with the pursuing Japanese soldiers, An was left with only three men with whom he wandered in the forests for several days, suffering from hunger and fatigue, barely managing to return to the maritime province. At one point, he was captured by a band of Koreans in the Manchurian hinterland who were about to turn him over to the Japanese. Not all Koreans were patriotically minded. In Vladivostok, he learned of Ito's forthcoming visit, went to Harbin with an accomplice, Wu Tŏk-sun, and succeeded in shooting Ito at the Harbin Railroad Station on October 26, 1909. He was hailed by many nationalists as a hero, but others expressed fears about Japanese retaliation against the Korean people.

In the course of his trial, An Chung-gŭn articulated the grievances of Koreans against Japan in general and against Ito Hirobumi in particular. An Chung-gŭn also engaged in heated debates with the prosecutors about the rights and wrongs of Japanese policy toward Korea. In essence, An argued that Ito destroyed the chance for peace in East Asia by selfishly acting to take over Korea. While Japan did improve Korea's sanitation, transportation, and education as the prosecutors argued, An replied that these improvements were designed for Japan's interests rather than Korea's. If Japan had provided support to Korea and honored its promise of protecting Korea's independence rather than making it a colony, An Chung-gŭn argued, Korea would have advanced on its own just as Japan had advanced from its backwardness. Furthermore, Ito engaged in falsehood by announcing that the protectorate treaty of 1905 and the treaty of 1907 were concluded at the demand of the Korean people. An Chung-gŭn repeatedly asserted that he was not a simple assassin but a Lieutenant General of the Righteous Army engaged in destroying the enemy. His fate, however, had been decided beforehand by the government in Tokyo rather than by the judges in Port Arthur.

Most of the interrogations are devoted to the prosecutors' attempts to discover An's accomplices and An's attempts to shield others. But, occasionally, the prosecutors attempted to persuade An Chung-gŭn to accept Japanese points of view about Korea. To the end, however, An remained unpersuaded. In the course of these "debates," An revealed his depth of knowledge about world affairs and the developments in Japan and Korea. Even though An Chung-gŭn was put to death by the Japanese captors, he left two pieces of calligraphy to the prosecutors who had interrogated him. Such civility, of course, was not to be observed in subsequent years.

As I have stated earlier, there is much to be gained by pondering the meaning of An Chung-gŭn's action. Even though the times and circumstances have changed, many questions of similar nature are still neither discussed nor resolved. Professor Ichikawa, who has previously edited numerous works of importance on Japanese-Korean relations and Japan's rule of Korea, has rendered a valuable service by making these new materials available. It should be a required reading for all those interested in Japanese-Korean relations.

Chong-Sik Lee<br>
University of Pennsylvania

*Korean Studies,* a serial publication of scholarly writing on Korea, is published for the Center for Korean Studies by The University Press of Hawaii. The Center for Korean Studies was established in 1972 to coordinate and develop the resources for the study of Korea at the University of Hawaii. Its goals are the enhancement of faculty quality and performance in Korean studies, the development of comprehensive and balanced academic programs, and the stimulation of research and publication. The Center seeks especially to promote interdisciplinary and intercultural studies.

The Center for Korean Studies welcomes scholarly articles dealing with Korea in all academic disciplines. All articles will be printed in English. Manuscripts should be prepared in accordance with *A Manual of Style, Twelfth Edition, Revised* (Chicago and London: University of Chicago Press, 1969). Transliteration of Korean should conform to the McCune-Reischauer system, except that the Yale romanization system may be used in articles in linguistics. Contributions should be addressed to The Center for Korean Studies, University of Hawaii, 1881 East-West Road, Honolulu, Hawaii 96822.

Payment with order is requested. Orders should be addressed to The University Press of Hawaii, 2840 Kolowalu Street, Honolulu, Hawaii 96822 USA.

Articles appearing in this journal are abstracted and indexed in *Historical Abstracts* and *America: History and Life.*

# DATE DUE